SBA Commercial Mortgage Loan Fundamentals

Understanding SBA Mortgage Programs, Requirements, and How to Qualify for Approval

By Joseph G. Correa

Licensed Mortgage Broker, Finibi Mortgage

Copyright & Legal Notice

Published by Live Stronger Faster

The information provided in this book is for educational and informational purposes only and does not constitute financial, legal, tax, or investment advice. Although the author is a licensed mortgage professional, the content presented is general in nature and is not intended as personalized guidance for any specific individual, business, or financial situation.

The strategies, loan structures, and examples discussed in this book are illustrative and educational in nature. They are intended to demonstrate concepts related to SBA commercial mortgage financing, including SBA 7(a) and 504 loan programs, borrower qualification, debt service coverage analysis, property acquisition, refinancing, construction financing, and advanced loan structuring. These examples do not represent guaranteed approvals, loan terms, or outcomes. Results may vary significantly based on individual financial profiles, credit history, business performance, property type, market conditions, and lender-specific guidelines.

SBA loan programs are subject to eligibility requirements, regulatory guidelines, and changes established by the U.S. Small Business Administration and participating lenders. Borrowers are encouraged to consult directly with qualified financial, legal, and tax professionals before making any financing or investment decisions.

The author and publisher make no representations or warranties regarding the accuracy, completeness, or applicability of the content and disclaim any liability for errors, omissions, or outcomes resulting from the use or misuse of the information contained in this book.

First Edition, 2026

Table of Contents

Introduction

The world of commercial real estate and business ownership has traditionally been dominated by those with substantial capital, long-standing banking relationships, and access to sophisticated financing structures. For many aspiring entrepreneurs, investors, and business owners, the idea of purchasing a commercial property, acquiring a business with real estate, or expanding into a larger facility can feel out of reach. However, there is a powerful and often underutilized pathway that has helped millions of individuals bridge this gap and step into ownership: SBA commercial mortgage financing.

The U.S. Small Business Administration was created with a clear mission—to empower small businesses by improving access to capital. Through its lending programs, the SBA does not directly issue loans but instead partners with approved lenders to guarantee a portion of the loan. This guarantee significantly reduces risk for lenders, making it easier for borrowers to qualify for financing that might otherwise be unavailable through conventional channels. What this means for you, as a reader of this series, is that SBA mortgage programs open doors that traditional commercial loans often keep closed. This book, *SBA Commercial Mortgage Loan Fundamentals*, serves as your foundation for understanding how these programs work, who they are designed for, and how you can position yourself for approval. Whether you are an entrepreneur looking to buy your first business property, a self-employed borrower seeking stability, or an investor planning to scale strategically, this introduction is your gateway into a system that can transform your financial trajectory.

At its core, SBA commercial mortgage financing is about access and opportunity. Unlike conventional commercial loans that may require high down payments, strict underwriting standards, and extensive documentation, SBA loans are structured with flexibility in mind. Programs such as the SBA 7(a) and SBA 504 loans are specifically designed to support owner-occupied businesses, allowing borrowers to finance not only the real estate but also the operations tied to that property. This unique combination of business and real estate financing creates a powerful leverage point for growth.

One of the most important distinctions you will learn throughout this series is the concept of owner occupancy. SBA mortgage loans are primarily intended for businesses that will occupy at least 51% of the property. This requirement aligns with the SBA's mission to support active businesses rather than passive real estate investments. However, within this framework lies tremendous opportunity. By occupying a portion of the property, you can generate income from the remaining space, effectively turning your business location into a hybrid asset that supports both operations and investment growth.

As you progress through this book, you will begin to understand how SBA loans evaluate borrowers differently from conventional financing. Instead of focusing solely on credit scores and collateral, SBA underwriting takes a broader view of your business, your experience, your cash flow, and your ability to repay the loan over time. This holistic approach allows borrowers with non-traditional financial profiles to qualify, including those who are self-employed, transitioning careers, or rebuilding their financial foundation.

Another defining feature of SBA commercial mortgage loans is the structure of the financing itself. These loans often come with longer repayment terms—up to 25 years for real estate—which significantly reduces monthly payments compared to shorter-term commercial loans. Lower payments improve cash flow, and improved cash flow creates stability, scalability, and resilience for your business. This is not just about qualifying for a loan; it is about setting up a financial structure that supports long-term success.

Throughout this series, you will also discover how SBA financing can be used in a variety of strategic ways. You can purchase an existing commercial property, refinance high-interest debt, acquire a business that includes real estate, or even construct a new building tailored to your operational needs. Each of these strategies will be explored in depth in the books that follow, but it is important to recognize from the beginning that SBA mortgage financing is not a one-size-fits-all solution—it is a flexible toolkit that can be adapted to your specific goals.

In today's evolving economic landscape, where interest rates fluctuate and lending standards shift, having access to a government-backed financing option provides a level of stability and predictability that is difficult to find elsewhere. SBA loans often feature competitive interest rates and structured terms that are designed to remain sustainable over time. This makes them particularly attractive for long-term investments and business planning.

However, while SBA loans offer tremendous advantages, they are not without their requirements. Borrowers must demonstrate a viable business purpose, sufficient cash flow, and a reasonable level of financial responsibility. There are also documentation requirements, including financial statements, tax returns, and business plans, that must be carefully prepared and presented. This book will guide you through these requirements step by step, helping you understand not only what is needed but why it matters and how to position yourself effectively.

One of the most empowering aspects of SBA commercial mortgage financing is that it allows you to control your future rather than rent it. Instead of paying rent to a landlord and building someone else's wealth, you can own the property your business operates in, build equity over time, and create an asset that appreciates in value. This shift from tenant to owner is one of the most significant financial transformations a business owner can make.

As you move through this introduction and into the chapters that follow, you will begin to see how SBA loans fit into a larger strategy of wealth creation and business expansion. Ownership leads to equity. Equity leads to leverage. Leverage leads to opportunity. And opportunity, when managed correctly, leads to long-term financial independence.

This series has been designed not just to educate you, but to empower you with actionable knowledge. Each book builds upon the last, taking you from foundational concepts to advanced structuring strategies. By the time you reach Book 10, you will have a comprehensive understanding of how to structure complex SBA mortgage deals, navigate underwriting challenges, and maximize your chances of approval. But everything starts here—with the fundamentals. Understanding how SBA mortgage programs work is the first step toward using them effectively. In this book, you will learn about the key loan programs, eligibility requirements, underwriting criteria, and approval process. You will gain clarity on what lenders are looking for and how to present yourself as a strong borrower.

You will also begin to develop a new mindset around financing. Instead of seeing loans as obstacles or risks, you will learn to view them as tools—tools that, when used correctly, can accelerate your growth and unlock opportunities that would otherwise remain out of reach. This shift in perspective is critical, because success in commercial real estate and business ownership is not just about knowledge; it is about how you apply that knowledge strategically.

As you read, imagine the possibilities. Imagine owning the building your business operates in. Imagine acquiring a profitable business with real estate included. Imagine expanding into multiple locations, each supported by structured financing that enhances your cash flow rather than constrains it. These are not distant goals—they are achievable outcomes when you understand and leverage SBA commercial mortgage loans effectively. This introduction marks the beginning of that journey. It is your entry point into a system designed to support growth, ownership, and long-term success. The path ahead will require focus, discipline, and strategic thinking, but the rewards are substantial. With the right knowledge and execution, SBA mortgage financing can become one of the most powerful tools in your financial arsenal.

Welcome to *The SBA Commercial Mortgage Loan Mastery Series*. Your journey toward ownership, expansion, and financial control starts now.

Chapter 1

Understanding SBA Commercial Mortgage Loan Programs and How They Work

SBA commercial mortgage loan programs represent one of the most powerful and flexible financing tools available to business owners and entrepreneurs who want to acquire, refinance, or build commercial real estate tied to their operations. At the center of this system is the U.S. Small Business Administration, which provides guarantees to approved lenders, reducing their risk and enabling borrowers to access capital under more favorable terms than conventional commercial loans. To fully understand how to leverage SBA mortgage financing, it is essential to break down the structure, purpose, and mechanics of these programs, particularly the SBA 7(a) and SBA 504 loan options, which dominate the commercial real estate landscape.

The SBA 7(a) loan program is the most versatile and widely used option within SBA financing. It allows borrowers to use funds for a variety of purposes, including purchasing commercial real estate, acquiring a business, refinancing debt, and covering working capital needs. When used for real estate, the SBA 7(a) program becomes a powerful hybrid loan that combines property acquisition with business financing. This flexibility is particularly beneficial for entrepreneurs who are not only purchasing a building but also investing in the growth and operation of their business. The SBA guarantees a portion of the loan—typically up to 75%—which significantly reduces lender risk and opens the door for borrowers who may not qualify under traditional underwriting standards.

In contrast, the SBA 504 loan program is designed specifically for long-term, fixed-asset financing, particularly commercial real estate and large equipment purchases. The structure of a 504 loan is unique because it involves two separate lenders: a traditional bank or lender that provides approximately 50% of the financing, and a Certified Development Company (CDC) that provides up to 40%, with the borrower contributing as little as 10% as a down payment. This layered structure allows borrowers to access long-term, fixed-rate financing on a significant portion of the loan, often resulting in more predictable payments and reduced interest rate risk over time.

One of the defining characteristics of SBA commercial mortgage loans is the owner-occupancy requirement. Unlike conventional investment property loans, SBA loans require that the borrower's business occupy at least 51% of the property for existing buildings, or 60% for new construction.

This requirement aligns with the SBA's mission to support active businesses rather than passive real estate investors. However, this does not eliminate the potential for investment income. Borrowers can lease out the remaining space, creating an additional revenue stream that can enhance the overall financial performance of the property.

Another critical component of SBA loan programs is the concept of cash flow-based underwriting. Rather than relying solely on collateral value or borrower net worth, SBA lenders focus heavily on the business's ability to generate sufficient income to repay the loan. This is typically measured through a debt service coverage ratio (DSCR), which compares the business's net operating income to its total debt obligations. A DSCR of 1.25 or higher is generally considered acceptable, meaning the business generates at least 25% more income than required to cover its debt payments. This emphasis on cash flow allows borrowers with strong businesses but limited assets to qualify for financing.

The terms and repayment structures of SBA commercial mortgage loans are another major advantage. Real estate loans under SBA programs can extend up to 25 years, significantly lowering monthly payments compared to shorter-term commercial loans. This extended amortization period improves cash flow, making it easier for businesses to manage expenses and reinvest in growth. Additionally, interest rates on SBA loans are often competitive, with options for both fixed and variable rates depending on the program and lender.

SBA loans also provide flexibility in how funds are used within a transaction. For example, a borrower purchasing a business that includes real estate can use an SBA 7(a) loan to finance both the acquisition of the business and the property in a single loan. This eliminates the need for multiple financing sources and simplifies the overall transaction. Similarly, SBA loans can be used for refinancing existing debt, provided that the refinance results in a tangible benefit to the borrower, such as reduced payments or improved cash flow.

Despite their advantages, SBA commercial mortgage loans come with specific eligibility requirements that borrowers must meet. These include operating as a for-profit business, meeting size standards defined by the SBA, demonstrating a sound business purpose, and showing the ability to repay the loan. Borrowers must also typically provide a personal guarantee, meaning they are personally responsible for the loan if the business cannot repay it. This requirement underscores the importance of careful planning and financial management when pursuing SBA financing.

Documentation plays a significant role in the SBA loan process. Borrowers are required to provide detailed financial information, including personal and business tax returns, profit and loss statements, balance sheets, and projections. Lenders use this information to assess the borrower's financial health, stability, and capacity for repayment. While this level of documentation may seem extensive, it also provides an opportunity for borrowers to present a strong case for approval by demonstrating the viability and profitability of their business.

Another key aspect of SBA commercial mortgage loans is the timeline. Compared to conventional loans, SBA loans may take longer to process due to the additional documentation and underwriting requirements. However, this timeline can be managed effectively with proper preparation and organization. Working with experienced lenders and understanding the process in advance can significantly reduce delays and improve the overall experience.

As you begin to understand how SBA commercial mortgage loan programs work, it becomes clear that these loans are not just about financing—they are about strategy. They allow business owners to transition from renting to owning, to build equity, and to create long-term financial stability. By leveraging the structure, flexibility, and support provided by

SBA programs, borrowers can achieve goals that might otherwise be out of reach. This chapter lays the foundation for everything that follows in this series. By understanding the core programs, requirements, and structures of SBA commercial mortgage loans, you are now positioned to explore more advanced strategies in the chapters ahead. The knowledge you gain here will serve as the framework for making informed decisions, structuring successful deals, and ultimately achieving approval for SBA financing.

Real-Life Math Example: SBA Commercial Mortgage Loan Scenario

To fully understand how SBA commercial mortgage loans work in practice, let's walk through a detailed real-life scenario that illustrates the numbers, structure, and financial impact of an SBA loan.

Imagine a business owner named Carlos who operates a successful logistics company generating $300,000 in annual net income. Carlos currently rents a warehouse space for $6,000 per month, totaling $72,000 per year in rent expenses. He wants to purchase a commercial property for $1,200,000 to house his business and reduce long-term costs while building equity.

Carlos decides to pursue an SBA 504 loan. The structure of the loan breaks down as follows: 50% from a bank ($600,000), 40% from a CDC ($480,000), and a 10% down payment from Carlos ($120,000). This allows Carlos to acquire the property with a relatively low upfront investment compared to conventional financing, which might require 20% to 30% down.

The bank portion of $600,000 is financed at a 6.5% interest rate over 25 years, resulting in a monthly payment of approximately $4,050. The CDC portion of $480,000 is financed at a fixed rate of 5.5% over 25 years, resulting in a monthly payment of approximately $2,950. Combined, Carlos's total monthly mortgage payment is $7,000.

At first glance, this appears slightly higher than his current rent of $6,000 per month. However, this comparison does not tell the full story. Of the $7,000 monthly payment, a portion goes toward principal, meaning Carlos is building equity in the property with each payment. Additionally, commercial properties often appreciate over time, increasing the value of his investment.

Now let's analyze Carlos's debt service coverage ratio (DSCR). His annual mortgage payments total $84,000 ($7,000 x 12). With a net income of $300,000, his DSCR is calculated as

$300,000 divided by $84,000, which equals approximately 3.57. This is well above the typical minimum requirement of 1.25, indicating strong cash flow and a high likelihood of loan approval. Carlos also has the option to lease out 20% of the property to another business, generating an additional $2,000 per month in rental income. This reduces his effective monthly cost from $7,000 to $5,000, making his ownership cost lower than his previous rent. Over time, this additional income further strengthens his financial position and increases the overall return on investment.

Over a 10-year period, Carlos will have paid down a significant portion of the loan principal. Assuming modest property appreciation of 3% per year, the $1,200,000 property could increase in value to approximately $1,612,000. Combined with principal reduction, Carlos could build several hundred thousand dollars in equity, transforming his business expense into a wealth-building asset.

This example demonstrates the power of SBA commercial mortgage loans. By leveraging a relatively small down payment and structured financing, Carlos is able to transition from renting to owning, improve his long-term financial position, and create additional income streams. The numbers tell a clear story: SBA financing is not just about qualifying for a loan—it is about using that loan strategically to build wealth, stability, and opportunity over time.

As you continue through this book and the series, you will learn how to structure similar deals, analyze financial scenarios, and position yourself for approval. The key is understanding both the mechanics and the strategy behind SBA commercial mortgage loans, and applying that knowledge to your unique situation.

Chapter 2

SBA Commercial Mortgage Loan Eligibility Requirements and Borrower Qualification

Understanding SBA commercial mortgage loan eligibility is one of the most critical steps in securing approval and successfully leveraging these programs for business growth and real estate ownership. While SBA loans are designed to be more flexible than conventional financing, they are still governed by a structured set of requirements that ensure borrowers are capable of repaying the loan and operating a sustainable business. In this chapter, we will break down the key eligibility factors, how lenders evaluate borrowers, and how you can position yourself strategically to meet and exceed these requirements.

At the foundation of SBA loan eligibility is the requirement that the borrower operates a for-profit business. The U.S. Small Business Administration does not support nonprofit entities through its standard loan programs, as its mission is focused on stimulating economic growth through small business expansion. In addition to being for-profit, the business must meet SBA size standards, which vary by industry and are typically based on either annual revenue or number of employees. These standards ensure that SBA programs are targeted toward small and mid-sized businesses rather than large corporations.

Another core eligibility requirement is that the borrower must demonstrate a sound business purpose for the loan. This means the funds must be used for legitimate business activities such as purchasing commercial real estate, acquiring a business, refinancing existing debt, or funding construction and expansion. Lenders will carefully review the intended use of funds to ensure alignment with SBA guidelines. This is not just a formality; it is a critical part of the underwriting process that determines whether the loan qualifies for SBA backing.

One of the most important borrower qualifications is creditworthiness. While SBA loans are more forgiving than conventional loans, lenders still expect borrowers to have a reasonable credit profile. This includes both personal and business credit. A strong personal credit score—typically 680 or higher—can significantly improve approval chances, but borrowers with lower scores may still qualify if they can demonstrate strong compensating factors such as stable income, significant experience, or strong cash flow. The SBA does not set a strict minimum credit score, but lenders use credit as an indicator of financial responsibility and risk.

Cash flow is arguably the most critical component of SBA loan qualification. Lenders evaluate whether the business generates enough income to cover its debt obligations, including the proposed loan. This is measured using the debt service coverage ratio (DSCR), which compares net operating income to total debt payments. A DSCR of 1.25 or higher is generally required, meaning the business generates at least 25% more income than needed to cover its debts. However, stronger DSCR ratios—such as 1.5 or higher—can significantly improve approval odds and may even lead to better loan terms.

In addition to cash flow, lenders assess the borrower's experience and management capability. SBA loans are designed to support businesses that are likely to succeed, and one of the strongest indicators of success is the borrower's background in the industry. For example, a borrower with several years of experience operating a similar business will be viewed more favorably than someone entering a completely new industry. This does not mean that new entrepreneurs cannot qualify, but they may need to provide additional support, such as hiring experienced management or presenting a strong business plan.

Collateral is another factor in SBA loan qualification, although it is not always a deal-breaker. SBA loans are considered cash flow loans, meaning they are primarily based on the borrower's ability to repay rather than the value of collateral. However, lenders will still seek to secure the loan with available assets, including the commercial property being financed and, in some cases, personal assets. If there is a shortfall in collateral, the SBA guarantee helps mitigate the risk, allowing the loan to move forward in many cases.

A unique aspect of SBA loans is the personal guarantee requirement. All owners with 20% or more ownership in the business are typically required to personally guarantee the loan. This means they are personally responsible for repayment if the business defaults. While this may seem like a significant commitment, it also demonstrates to lenders that the borrower is fully invested in the success of the business. This alignment of interests is a key factor in SBA underwriting.

Liquidity and reserves also play an important role in borrower qualification. Lenders want to see that borrowers have sufficient cash reserves to cover unexpected expenses and maintain operations during periods of reduced revenue. This may include several months of loan payments in reserve, as well as additional working capital. Strong liquidity can serve as a compensating factor for other areas, such as lower credit scores or limited collateral.

The borrower's financial history is also carefully reviewed, including past bankruptcies, foreclosures, or delinquencies. While these events do not automatically disqualify a borrower, they must be explained and resolved. Lenders will look for evidence that the borrower has recovered financially and established a pattern of responsible behavior. Transparency and documentation are critical in these situations.

Another key eligibility factor is the owner-occupancy requirement for commercial real estate. As discussed in Chapter 1, SBA loans require that the borrower's business occupy at least 51% of the property. This ensures that the loan is used to support active business operations rather than passive investment. Borrowers must be prepared to demonstrate how the property will be used and how it supports their business activities.

Documentation is a central part of the qualification process. Borrowers must provide comprehensive financial records, including personal and business tax returns, profit and loss statements, balance sheets, and financial projections. A well-prepared loan package can significantly improve approval chances by clearly demonstrating the strength and viability of the business. This is where many borrowers either strengthen or weaken their application, depending on how well they present their financial story. Ultimately, SBA loan eligibility is about more than meeting minimum requirements—it is about presenting a complete and compelling picture of your business and your ability to succeed. Lenders are not just evaluating numbers; they are evaluating risk, potential, and long-term viability. By understanding these factors and preparing accordingly, you can position yourself as a strong candidate for SBA financing.

This chapter provides the blueprint for qualification. As you move forward in this series, you will learn how to take these requirements and turn them into actionable strategies that increase your chances of approval and help you structure successful deals.

Real-Life Math Example: SBA Loan Qualification and DSCR Analysis

Let's walk through a detailed real-life scenario to understand how SBA loan eligibility is evaluated using actual numbers.

Imagine a borrower named Maria who owns a small manufacturing business. Her business generates $250,000 in annual net operating income. Maria wants to purchase a commercial property for $900,000 using an SBA 7(a) loan. She plans to put down 10%, or $90,000, and finance the remaining $810,000.

The loan is structured with a 25-year term at an interest rate of

7%. Based on these terms, Maria's monthly payment is approximately $5,730, which results in an annual debt service of $68,760.

To determine whether Maria qualifies, the lender calculates her debt service coverage ratio (DSCR). This is done by dividing her net operating income by her total annual debt payments. In this case, $250,000 divided by $68,760 equals approximately 3.63. This is well above the minimum requirement of 1.25, indicating strong cash flow and a high likelihood of approval.

However, Maria also has an existing business loan with annual payments of $20,000. This must be included in the total debt calculation. Her new total annual debt service becomes $88,760. When we recalculate the DSCR using this figure, $250,000 divided by $88,760 equals approximately 2.82. This is still a strong ratio and demonstrates that Maria's business can comfortably support the new loan.

Next, the lender evaluates Maria's liquidity. She has $120,000 in savings after her down payment, which is equivalent to approximately 16 months of loan payments. This strong reserve position further strengthens her application and provides a safety net for unexpected challenges.

Maria's credit score is 690, which is considered acceptable for

SBA financing. She has no recent delinquencies, and her financial history shows consistent improvement over the past five years. This positive trend supports her overall creditworthiness.

The lender also reviews the property and confirms that Maria's business will occupy 70% of the space, meeting the SBA's owner-occupancy requirement. She plans to lease out the remaining 30%, generating an additional $1,500 per month, or $18,000 per year, in rental income. This income can be considered as a compensating factor and may even be partially included in the cash flow analysis.

When all factors are combined—strong DSCR, sufficient liquidity, acceptable credit, relevant business experience, and compliance with SBA requirements—Maria's loan application is positioned for approval.

Now let's analyze the long-term impact. Over 10 years, Maria will pay down a significant portion of the loan principal. Assuming the property appreciates at 3% annually, the $900,000 property could be worth approximately $1,209,000 after 10 years. Combined with principal reduction, Maria could build over $400,000 in equity.

Additionally, the rental income of $18,000 per year offsets her loan payments, effectively reducing her net cost of ownership.

This demonstrates how SBA financing not only enables property acquisition but also creates opportunities for income generation and wealth building. This example highlights the importance of understanding SBA eligibility requirements and how they translate into real-world financial scenarios. By mastering these concepts, you can confidently evaluate your own situation, structure deals effectively, and position yourself for approval in the SBA loan process.

Chapter 3

Owner-Occupied Property Financing with SBA Commercial Mortgage Loans

Owner-occupied commercial real estate is the cornerstone of SBA commercial mortgage financing, and understanding how this concept works is essential to unlocking the full power of SBA loan programs. At its core, owner occupancy means that the business applying for the loan must physically operate within the property being financed. This requirement is central to the mission of the U.S. Small Business Administration, which is to support active businesses that contribute to economic growth, job creation, and long-term stability. Unlike conventional commercial real estate loans that often focus on passive investment properties, SBA loans are designed to empower business owners to control their operating environment while simultaneously building equity.

The owner-occupancy requirement is straightforward but powerful. For existing buildings, the borrower's business must occupy at least 51% of the total square footage. For new construction, the requirement increases to 60% occupancy, with plans to eventually occupy up to 80% over time. This structure ensures that the primary purpose of the loan is to support the borrower's business operations rather than purely investment-driven activities. However, within this framework lies a significant opportunity: borrowers can lease out the remaining portion of the property to generate additional income, effectively turning their commercial space into a hybrid asset that combines operational efficiency with investment potential.

One of the most transformative aspects of owner-occupied financing is the shift from leasing to owning. Many business owners spend years paying rent, often with annual increases and limited control over their space. These payments build no equity and provide no long-term financial benefit beyond the immediate use of the property. In contrast, SBA commercial mortgage loans allow business owners to convert what was once an expense into an asset. Each mortgage payment contributes to principal reduction, gradually increasing ownership and net worth over time.

Control is another major advantage of owner-occupied property financing. When you own your building, you eliminate the uncertainty associated with lease renewals, rent increases, and landlord restrictions. You can customize the property to meet your specific business needs, whether that involves renovations, expansions, or specialized equipment installations. This level of control can significantly enhance operational efficiency and create a more stable environment for growth.

From a financial perspective, owner-occupied SBA loans are structured to support long-term sustainability. With loan terms extending up to 25 years, monthly payments are often comparable to—or even lower than—market rent. This extended amortization reduces the financial burden on the business and improves cash flow, allowing for reinvestment in operations, marketing, staffing, and expansion. Over time, as inflation drives rental costs higher, fixed mortgage payments can become increasingly advantageous.

Another key benefit is the ability to leverage unused space within the property. For example, a business that occupies 60% of a building can lease the remaining 40% to other tenants. This rental income can offset mortgage payments, reduce operating costs, and improve overall profitability. In some cases, the income generated from tenants can cover a substantial portion of the mortgage, effectively allowing the business owner to operate at a reduced net cost.

SBA owner-occupied financing also provides strategic flexibility for future growth. As a business expands, it may gradually take over more of the building, reducing reliance on tenants and increasing operational capacity. Alternatively, if the business relocates or scales beyond the property, the building can be converted into a full investment property, creating a new income stream. This adaptability makes owner-occupied real estate a powerful long-term asset.

The underwriting process for owner-occupied properties focuses heavily on the business's ability to support the loan. Lenders evaluate cash flow, stability, and growth potential to ensure that the business can comfortably meet its debt obligations. This is typically measured using the debt service coverage ratio (DSCR), which compares net operating income to total debt payments. A strong DSCR not only increases the likelihood of approval but also provides a financial cushion that protects the business during periods of economic uncertainty.

Location and property type also play a role in owner-occupied financing. Lenders assess whether the property aligns with the business's operational needs and whether it has long-term value. Properties in strong commercial areas with stable demand are generally viewed more favorably, as they provide additional security for the loan. However, SBA loans are flexible enough to accommodate a wide range of property types, including office buildings, warehouses, retail spaces, and specialized facilities.

Another important consideration is the down payment requirement. SBA loans typically require a lower down payment compared to conventional commercial loans, often as low as 10%. This allows business owners to preserve capital for other uses, such as working capital, renovations, or expansion. By minimizing the upfront investment, SBA financing makes ownership more accessible and reduces the barrier to entry for many borrowers.

Tax advantages further enhance the appeal of owner-occupied real estate. Mortgage interest and property depreciation can often be deducted, reducing the overall tax burden for the business. These benefits, combined with equity growth and potential appreciation, create a powerful financial strategy that extends beyond the immediate benefits of ownership.

Risk management is also an important aspect of owner-occupied financing. While owning a property provides stability and long-term benefits, it also requires careful planning and financial discipline. Business owners must ensure that they maintain sufficient reserves, manage expenses effectively, and plan for potential changes in market conditions. SBA loans are structured to support stability, but success ultimately depends on how well the borrower manages the asset.

As you continue through this chapter, it becomes clear that owner-occupied SBA commercial mortgage loans are not just about acquiring property—they are about transforming the financial foundation of your business. They provide a pathway to ownership, control, and long-term wealth creation, all while supporting the day-to-day operations of your business.

This concept is at the heart of SBA financing. By aligning business operations with real estate ownership, borrowers can create a powerful synergy that drives growth, stability, and financial independence. Understanding how to leverage this strategy effectively is a key step toward mastering SBA commercial mortgage loans.

Real-Life Math Example: Owner-Occupied SBA Commercial Mortgage Scenario

Let's walk through a detailed real-life example to illustrate how owner-occupied SBA financing works in practice.

Imagine a business owner named David who operates a growing auto repair company. His business generates $280,000 in annual net operating income, and he currently rents a facility for $5,500 per month, or $66,000 per year. David has found a commercial property for $1,000,000 that would allow him to expand his operations while also providing additional space for rental income.

David decides to use an SBA 7(a) loan with a 10% down payment of $100,000, financing the remaining $900,000. The loan is structured over 25 years at an interest rate of 6.75%, resulting in a monthly payment of approximately $6,200, or $74,400 annually.

At first glance, David's new payment is higher than his current rent. However, this comparison changes when we consider the full financial picture. David plans to occupy 60% of the building and lease out the remaining 40% to two tenants, generating $2,500 per month in rental income, or $30,000 annually.

This rental income reduces David's effective annual cost from $74,400 to $44,400. Compared to his previous rent of $66,000, David is now saving $21,600 per year while also building equity in the property.

Next, we calculate David's debt service coverage ratio (DSCR). His total annual debt payment is $74,400. With a net operating income of $280,000, his DSCR is calculated as $280,000 divided by $74,400, which equals approximately 3.76. This is well above the minimum requirement of 1.25, indicating strong financial capacity.

Over time, David's financial position continues to improve. Assuming a modest property appreciation rate of 3% annually, the $1,000,000 property could be worth approximately $1,343,000 after 10 years. During this same period, David will have paid down a significant portion of the loan principal, potentially building over $400,000 in equity.

Additionally, rental income may increase over time due to market conditions, further reducing David's net cost of ownership. If rental income increases to $3,000 per month, his annual rental income would rise to $36,000, reducing his effective cost even further.

This example demonstrates the power of owner-occupied SBA financing. By combining business operations with real estate ownership, David is able to reduce expenses, generate additional income, and build long-term wealth. Instead of paying rent with no return, he is investing in an asset that grows in value and supports his business.

The numbers clearly illustrate the strategic advantage of SBA owner-occupied loans. They are not just a financing tool—they are a pathway to financial control, stability, and long-term success.

Chapter 4

Buying a Business and Real Estate with SBA Commercial Mortgage Financing

One of the most powerful and strategic uses of SBA commercial mortgage loans is the ability to acquire both a business and the real estate it operates in within a single transaction. This dual acquisition strategy allows entrepreneurs and investors to step into an existing income-producing operation while simultaneously securing ownership of the underlying property. It is a unique advantage made possible through SBA financing programs, particularly those backed by the U.S. Small Business Administration, which are specifically designed to support small business growth, continuity, and ownership.

When you purchase a business that includes real estate, you are not just buying a physical structure—you are acquiring a functioning ecosystem. This includes the operations, customer base, revenue streams, systems, employees, and location. SBA financing allows these elements to be bundled together into one loan, eliminating the need for separate financing sources. This simplifies the transaction and creates a cohesive financial structure that aligns the success of the business with the ownership of the property. At the core of this strategy is the

SBA 7(a) loan program, which provides the flexibility needed to finance both tangible and intangible assets. Unlike the SBA 504 program, which is focused primarily on fixed assets like real estate, the 7(a) program allows borrowers to include goodwill, inventory, equipment, and working capital in the loan. This makes it the ideal vehicle for business acquisitions that include real estate. The ability to finance goodwill is particularly important, as it represents the value of the business beyond its physical assets—its brand, reputation, and earning potential.

One of the most important aspects of buying a business with real estate is understanding how value is determined. The total purchase price is typically divided into two main components: the value of the real estate and the value of the business. The real estate is appraised based on market comparables, location, and condition, while the business is valued based on its financial performance, typically using metrics such as EBITDA (earnings before interest, taxes, depreciation, and amortization). Lenders will analyze both components to ensure that the overall transaction is reasonable and supported by the business's cash flow.

Cash flow is the foundation of SBA loan approval, especially in business acquisition scenarios. Lenders want to see that the business generates sufficient income to cover the combined debt service of both the business and real estate portions of the loan. This is evaluated through the debt service coverage ratio (DSCR), which compares the business's net operating income to its total debt obligations. A strong DSCR indicates that the business can comfortably support the loan, reducing risk for both the lender and the borrower.

Another critical factor is the transition of ownership. When acquiring a business, lenders assess not only the financial performance of the business but also the borrower's ability to successfully operate it. This includes evaluating the borrower's experience, management skills, and understanding of the industry. In many cases, the seller may be required to provide transitional support for a period of time to ensure a smooth handover. This support can include training, consulting, and introductions to key customers and vendors.

The structure of the down payment is another important consideration. SBA loans typically require a minimum down payment of 10%, but this can vary depending on the specifics of the transaction. In some cases, a portion of the down payment can be financed through a seller note, which is a loan provided by the seller to the buyer. This not only reduces the upfront cash requirement but also demonstrates the seller's confidence in the continued success of the business.

One of the most compelling advantages of acquiring a business with real estate is the alignment of expenses and ownership. Instead of paying rent to a landlord, the business pays its mortgage, effectively converting an operating expense into an investment. Over time, this builds equity in the property while maintaining control over the business location. This alignment creates a powerful financial dynamic that supports long-term growth and stability.

Additionally, owning the real estate provides a hedge against rising rental costs. Commercial rents can increase significantly over time, especially in high-demand areas. By locking in a fixed or predictable mortgage payment, borrowers can protect themselves from these increases and maintain greater control over their operating expenses. This stability is particularly valuable for businesses with tight margins or long-term planning horizons.

SBA financing also allows for the inclusion of working capital in the loan, which can be critical during the transition period. When a new owner takes over a business, there are often initial expenses related to operations, marketing, staffing, and improvements. Having access to working capital ensures that the business can continue to operate smoothly without financial strain.

Risk management is an essential part of any business acquisition. While SBA loans provide significant advantages, they also require careful due diligence. Borrowers must thoroughly analyze the financials of the business, including revenue trends, expenses, customer concentration, and market conditions. Understanding these factors helps ensure that the acquisition is not only feasible but also sustainable.

Another key consideration is the potential for growth. When evaluating a business acquisition, it is important to look beyond current performance and consider future opportunities. This may include expanding services, increasing efficiency, or leveraging the property for additional income. SBA financing provides the flexibility to pursue these opportunities, making it a powerful tool for scaling a business.

Tax benefits also play a role in the overall financial strategy. Interest on the loan may be deductible, and depreciation of the property can provide additional tax advantages. These benefits can improve cash flow and enhance the overall return on investment.

As you move through this chapter, it becomes clear that buying a business with real estate using SBA financing is not just a transaction—it is a strategic move that combines income generation, asset ownership, and long-term wealth building. It allows borrowers to step into an established operation while simultaneously securing a valuable asset that appreciates over time.

This approach requires careful planning, analysis, and execution, but the rewards can be substantial. By understanding how to structure these deals and evaluate opportunities, you can position yourself to take advantage of one of the most powerful strategies in commercial real estate and business ownership.

Real-Life Math Example: Buying a Business and Real Estate with SBA Financing

Let's walk through a detailed real-life scenario to illustrate how these transactions work financially.

Imagine an entrepreneur named Lisa who wants to purchase a profitable daycare business that includes the building it operates in. The total purchase price is $1,500,000, with $900,000 allocated to the real estate and $600,000 attributed to the business, including goodwill, equipment, and established operations.

Lisa decides to use an SBA 7(a) loan with a 10% down payment of $150,000. She finances the remaining $1,350,000 over 25 years at an interest rate of 7%, resulting in a monthly payment of approximately $9,540, or $114,480 annually. The daycare business generates $350,000 in annual net operating income. To determine whether Lisa qualifies, the lender calculates the debt service coverage ratio (DSCR). This is done by dividing the net operating income by the annual debt service. In this case, $350,000 divided by $114,480 equals approximately 3.06, which is well above the minimum requirement of 1.25.

Lisa also benefits from the fact that she no longer has to pay rent, which was previously $6,000 per month, or $72,000 annually. This rent expense is now replaced by her mortgage payment, which includes both principal and interest. While the mortgage payment is higher, a portion of it goes toward building equity in the property.

Over time, Lisa's financial position improves significantly. Assuming the property appreciates at 3% annually, the $900,000 real estate portion could be worth approximately $1,209,000 after 10 years. During this same period, Lisa will have paid down a substantial portion of the loan principal, potentially building over $500,000 in combined equity.

Additionally, Lisa identifies an opportunity to lease out a small portion of the property to a tutoring service, generating $1,500 per month, or $18,000 annually. This additional income reduces her effective annual debt cost from $114,480 to $96,480, further improving her cash flow.

Let's break down the numbers further. Lisa's net operating income of $350,000 minus her adjusted debt service of $96,480 leaves her with $253,520 in remaining income before taxes and reinvestment. This strong cash flow provides flexibility for business growth, staffing, and improvements.

If Lisa increases enrollment and improves operations, she could potentially grow the business's net income to $400,000 annually. At that level, her DSCR would increase even further, strengthening her financial position and creating opportunities for future expansion or refinancing.

This example demonstrates how SBA financing can be used to acquire both a business and real estate in a single transaction, creating a powerful combination of income and asset ownership. By leveraging structured financing, Lisa is able to control a $1.5 million asset with a relatively small upfront investment, while generating strong cash flow and building long-term wealth.

The numbers tell a clear story: SBA loans are not just about access to capital—they are about using that capital strategically to create opportunities, stability, and financial growth.

Chapter 5

SBA 7(a) Mortgage Loan Strategies for Commercial Financing

The SBA 7(a) loan program is widely recognized as the most flexible and powerful financing tool available to small business owners seeking to acquire, refinance, or expand commercial real estate tied to their operations. Backed by the U.S. Small Business Administration, this program provides a unique combination of accessibility, adaptability, and strategic potential that sets it apart from traditional commercial lending options. While many borrowers view SBA 7(a) loans simply as a way to secure funding, experienced investors and business owners understand that the true power of this program lies in how it is structured and deployed.

At its core, the SBA 7(a) loan is designed to provide working capital and long-term financing under a single loan structure. This is particularly valuable in commercial real estate transactions, where borrowers often need funds not only for the property itself but also for associated costs such as business acquisition, equipment, inventory, tenant improvements, and operational reserves. Unlike the SBA 504 program, which is limited to fixed assets, the 7(a) program allows borrowers to bundle multiple financing needs into one cohesive structure. This reduces complexity, lowers closing costs, and creates a streamlined path to ownership and expansion.

One of the most important strategies when using SBA 7(a) financing is maximizing leverage while maintaining strong cash flow. With down payment requirements typically starting at 10%, borrowers can control large assets with relatively small upfront investments. However, leverage must be balanced with the ability to service the debt. This is where understanding and optimizing the debt service coverage ratio (DSCR) becomes critical. A strong DSCR not only improves approval chances but also provides a financial cushion that allows the business to withstand fluctuations in revenue.

Another key strategy involves structuring the loan to include working capital. Many borrowers underestimate the importance of liquidity during and after a transaction. By including working capital in the loan, borrowers can ensure that they have sufficient funds to cover operational expenses, marketing, staffing, and unexpected costs. This reduces financial stress during the transition period and allows the business to stabilize and grow more effectively.

Interest rate strategy is another critical component of SBA 7(a) financing. These loans often come with variable rates tied to a benchmark such as the prime rate. While this can result in lower initial payments compared to fixed-rate loans, it also introduces the risk of rate increases over time. Borrowers must evaluate their risk tolerance and consider strategies such as refinancing or paying down principal more aggressively to mitigate this risk. In some cases, lenders may offer fixed-rate options, which provide greater predictability but may come with slightly higher initial rates.

Prepayment considerations are also important when structuring SBA 7(a) loans. Many 7(a) loans include a prepayment penalty during the first few years, particularly for terms of 15 years or longer. This penalty typically decreases over time and is designed to protect lenders from early payoff. Borrowers should plan their exit or refinance strategy accordingly, ensuring that any potential savings from refinancing outweigh the cost of the penalty.

One of the most powerful strategies within the SBA 7(a) program is the ability to refinance existing debt. This can include high-interest business loans, credit lines, or even existing commercial mortgages. By consolidating debt into a single SBA loan with a longer term and lower rate, borrowers can significantly reduce their monthly payments and improve cash flow. This improved cash flow can then be reinvested into the business, creating a cycle of growth and expansion. SBA

7(a) loans also provide opportunities for value-add strategies. For example, a borrower may purchase a property that requires renovations or improvements and include those costs in the loan. By enhancing the property, the borrower can increase its value, improve operational efficiency, and potentially generate additional income through leasing unused space. This approach allows borrowers to create equity and increase returns without requiring additional capital.

Another advanced strategy involves combining business acquisition with real estate financing. As discussed in the previous chapter, the SBA 7(a) program allows borrowers to finance both components in a single loan. This creates a powerful synergy, as the income generated by the business supports the debt service, while the real estate provides long-term value and stability. This dual approach is particularly effective for entrepreneurs looking to step into established businesses with proven cash flow.

Credit optimization is another important factor in SBA 7(a) loan strategy. While the program is more flexible than conventional loans, borrowers with stronger credit profiles often receive better terms and faster approvals. This includes lower interest rates, reduced documentation requirements, and more favorable underwriting conditions. Borrowers should take steps to improve their credit before applying, such as reducing debt, correcting errors, and maintaining consistent payment histories.

Another key consideration is lender selection. Not all SBA lenders are the same, and choosing the right lender can significantly impact the outcome of the loan. Preferred SBA lenders have the authority to approve loans more quickly and may offer more flexible terms. Working with experienced lenders who understand your industry and goals can streamline the process and improve your chances of success.

Timing is also a critical factor in SBA 7(a) loan strategy. Market conditions, interest rates, and business performance all play a role in determining the optimal time to apply for financing. Borrowers should aim to secure financing when their business is performing well, as this strengthens their application and increases approval likelihood. Waiting until financial challenges arise can make the process more difficult and limit available options.

Risk management must also be considered when using SBA 7(a) financing. While leverage can amplify returns, it also increases exposure to risk. Borrowers must ensure that they maintain sufficient reserves, monitor cash flow closely, and plan for potential changes in market conditions. A well-structured SBA loan should support stability and growth, not create financial strain. As you move through this chapter, it becomes clear that the SBA 7(a) loan program is not just a financing option—it is a strategic tool that can be used to achieve a wide range of business and real estate goals. By understanding how to structure these loans effectively, borrowers can maximize leverage, improve cash flow, and create opportunities for long-term growth and wealth building.

This chapter provides a comprehensive framework for using SBA 7(a) loans strategically. As you continue through this series, you will build on this foundation, learning how to apply these strategies in increasingly complex scenarios and how to adapt them to your unique business objectives.

Real-Life Math Example: SBA 7(a) Loan Strategy in Action

Let's walk through a detailed real-life scenario to illustrate how SBA 7(a) loan strategies can be applied effectively.

Imagine a business owner named Robert who operates a growing fitness center. His business generates $320,000 in annual net operating income. He currently leases his space for $7,000 per month, or $84,000 annually. Robert wants to purchase a commercial property for $1,400,000 that will allow him to expand his operations and eliminate rent.

Robert uses an SBA 7(a) loan with a 10% down payment of $140,000, financing $1,260,000. The loan is structured over 25 years at an interest rate of 7.25%, resulting in a monthly payment of approximately $9,200, or $110,400 annually.

At first glance, Robert's mortgage payment is higher than his current rent. However, he includes $100,000 in working capital within the loan, allowing him to upgrade equipment, expand marketing, and improve operations. These improvements increase his annual net operating income from $320,000 to $380,000 within the first year.

Now let's calculate Robert's DSCR. His annual debt service is $110,400. With a net income of $380,000, his DSCR is approximately 3.44, which is well above the minimum requirement. This strong ratio demonstrates that the business can comfortably support the loan.

Robert also leases out 25% of the building to a physical therapy clinic, generating $2,500 per month, or $30,000 annually. This reduces his effective annual cost from $110,400 to $80,400, which is lower than his previous rent of $84,000.

Now let's analyze the long-term impact. Over 10 years, Robert will pay down a significant portion of the loan principal. Assuming a 3% annual appreciation rate, the $1,400,000 property could be worth approximately $1,879,000 after 10 years. Combined with principal reduction, Robert could build over $600,000 in equity. Additionally, Robert uses a portion of his increased cash flow to make extra principal payments of $1,000 per month. This accelerates loan payoff and reduces total interest paid over the life of the loan. Over time, this strategy further strengthens his financial position and increases his net worth.

Let's break down the numbers further. Robert's adjusted annual cost after rental income is $80,400. With a net income of $380,000, he has $299,600 remaining before taxes and reinvestment. This strong cash flow allows him to continue expanding his business and exploring additional opportunities.

If Robert decides to refinance after five years when interest rates drop, he may be able to reduce his rate to 6%. Even with a prepayment penalty, the long-term savings could outweigh the cost, further improving his financial position.

This example demonstrates how SBA 7(a) loans can be used strategically to achieve multiple goals: acquiring property, increasing income, reducing expenses, and building long-term wealth. By understanding and applying these strategies, borrowers can transform their financing into a powerful tool for growth and success.

Chapter 6

SBA 504 Mortgage Loans for Commercial Real Estate

The SBA 504 loan program is one of the most powerful tools available for business owners seeking long-term, stable, and cost-effective financing for commercial real estate. Unlike the more flexible SBA 7(a) program, which can be used for a wide range of purposes, the SBA 504 program is specifically designed for fixed-asset financing, including owner-occupied commercial real estate and large equipment purchases. Backed by the U.S. Small Business Administration, the 504 program provides a structured approach to financing that combines low down payments with long-term, fixed interest rates, making it an ideal solution for borrowers who prioritize stability and predictability.

At the heart of the SBA 504 loan structure is a unique partnership between three parties: a traditional lender (usually a bank), a Certified Development Company (CDC), and the borrower. The typical structure consists of 50% financing from the bank, 40% from the CDC, and a 10% down payment from the borrower. This layered approach allows borrowers to access substantial capital with relatively low upfront investment, while also benefiting from the fixed-rate portion of the CDC loan.

One of the most attractive features of the SBA 504 program is its long-term, fixed-rate financing. The CDC portion of the loan is typically fixed for 20 to 25 years, providing borrowers with predictable monthly payments that are not affected by fluctuations in interest rates. This stability is particularly valuable in uncertain economic environments, where rising rates can significantly impact cash flow. By locking in a fixed rate on a large portion of the loan, borrowers can plan with confidence and focus on growing their business.

The bank portion of the loan, which typically represents 50% of the total financing, may have either a fixed or variable rate depending on the lender and market conditions. While this introduces some variability, the overall structure still provides a high level of stability compared to fully variable-rate loans. Borrowers can also negotiate terms with the bank to align with their financial goals and risk tolerance.

Another key advantage of the SBA 504 program is the lower down payment requirement. Traditional commercial loans often require 20% to 30% down, which can be a significant barrier for many business owners. In contrast, the SBA 504 program typically requires only 10% down for standard transactions. This allows borrowers to preserve capital for other uses, such as working capital, renovations, or expansion. In some cases, the down payment may increase to 15% or 20% for special-use properties or startups, but it still remains lower than many conventional options.

The SBA 504 program is particularly well-suited for owner-occupied real estate, which must meet the SBA's occupancy requirements. As discussed in earlier chapters, the borrower's business must occupy at least 51% of the property for existing buildings or 60% for new construction. This ensures that the financing supports active business operations while still allowing for potential rental income from unused space.

One of the most powerful aspects of the SBA 504 loan is its impact on cash flow. By spreading payments over a long term and locking in a fixed rate, borrowers can significantly reduce their monthly obligations compared to shorter-term loans. This improved cash flow can be reinvested into the business, used to hire additional staff, expand operations, or build reserves. Over time, this creates a compounding effect that strengthens the business and enhances its long-term viability.

Another important benefit is the potential for property appreciation. Commercial real estate often increases in value over time, particularly in strong markets. By owning the property, borrowers can capture this appreciation and build equity, creating a valuable asset that contributes to their overall net worth. Combined with principal reduction from mortgage payments, this can result in significant wealth accumulation over the life of the loan.

The SBA 504 program also supports construction and renovation projects, making it a versatile tool for businesses that need customized spaces. Whether building a new facility from the ground up or upgrading an existing property, borrowers can include these costs in the loan, ensuring that the property meets their operational needs. This flexibility allows businesses to create environments that enhance efficiency, productivity, and customer experience.

However, the SBA 504 program is not without its requirements and limitations. Unlike the 7(a) program, it cannot be used for working capital, inventory, or business acquisition costs. It is strictly limited to fixed assets, which means borrowers must secure additional financing if they need funds for operational expenses. This distinction is important when deciding which SBA program best fits your needs.

The approval process for SBA 504 loans involves both the bank and the CDC, which can add complexity compared to a single-lender transaction. However, this dual approval process also provides additional oversight and support, ensuring that the loan is structured appropriately and meets SBA guidelines. Working with experienced lenders and CDCs can help streamline the process and improve the overall experience.

Risk management is another critical consideration. While the fixed-rate structure provides stability, borrowers must still ensure that their business generates sufficient cash flow to support the loan. This requires careful financial planning, accurate projections, and ongoing monitoring of performance. A well-structured SBA 504 loan should enhance stability, not create financial strain.

As you move through this chapter, it becomes clear that the SBA 504 loan program is a powerful tool for long-term commercial real estate financing. It provides a unique combination of low down payments, fixed rates, and extended terms that support stability and growth. For business owners seeking to control their operating environment and build long-term wealth, the 504 program offers a compelling solution.

This chapter lays the foundation for understanding how to use SBA 504 loans effectively. As you continue through this series, you will learn how to integrate this program into broader financing strategies and how to combine it with other tools to achieve your business and real estate goals.

Real-Life Math Example: SBA 504 Loan in Action

Let's walk through a detailed real-life scenario to illustrate how the SBA 504 loan program works financially.

Imagine a business owner named Angela who operates a successful manufacturing company generating $400,000 in annual net operating income. She wants to purchase a commercial property for $2,000,000 to expand her operations and eliminate her current lease, which costs $10,000 per month, or $120,000 annually.

Angela uses an SBA 504 loan with a 10% down payment of $200,000. The financing structure is as follows: $1,000,000 from a bank (50%), $800,000 from a CDC (40%), and $200,000 from Angela (10%).

The bank loan of $1,000,000 is financed at a 6.75% interest rate over 25 years, resulting in a monthly payment of approximately $6,900, or $82,800 annually. The CDC loan of $800,000 is financed at a fixed rate of 5.5% over 25 years, resulting in a monthly payment of approximately $4,900, or $58,800 annually.

Angela's total monthly payment is approximately $11,800, or

$141,600 annually. At first glance, this is higher than her current rent of $120,000 per year. However, this comparison changes when we consider the full financial picture.

Angela plans to lease out 20% of the property to another business, generating $3,000 per month, or $36,000 annually. This reduces her effective annual cost from $141,600 to $105,600, which is lower than her previous rent.

Next, we calculate Angela's debt service coverage ratio (DSCR). Her annual debt service is $141,600. With a net operating income of $400,000, her DSCR is approximately 2.83, which is well above the minimum requirement of 1.25. This indicates strong cash flow and a high likelihood of loan approval.

Over time, Angela's financial position improves significantly. Assuming a 3% annual appreciation rate, the $2,000,000 property could be worth approximately $2,686,000 after 10 years. During this same period, Angela will have paid down a substantial portion of the loan principal, potentially building over $800,000 in equity.

Additionally, the fixed-rate CDC portion of the loan protects Angela from rising interest rates, ensuring that a significant portion of her payments remains stable over time. This predictability allows her to plan for future growth and manage her finances more effectively. Let's break down the numbers further. Angela's adjusted annual cost after rental income is $105,600. With a net income of $400,000, she has $294,400 remaining before taxes and reinvestment. This strong cash flow provides flexibility for expansion, hiring, and additional investments.

If Angela increases her rental income over time or expands her business operations, her financial position will continue to improve. She may also have the option to refinance the bank portion of the loan in the future if interest rates decrease, further reducing her costs.

This example demonstrates how the SBA 504 loan program can be used to acquire commercial real estate, improve cash flow, and build long-term wealth. By leveraging structured financing and strategic planning, borrowers can transform their business expenses into valuable assets and create a foundation for sustained success.

Chapter 7

Refinancing Commercial Debt with SBA Mortgage Loans

Refinancing commercial debt using SBA mortgage loan programs is one of the most powerful yet often overlooked strategies available to business owners. While many entrepreneurs focus on using SBA loans for acquisitions or new purchases, the ability to refinance existing debt can be equally transformative. By restructuring high-interest loans, consolidating multiple obligations, or extending repayment terms, borrowers can significantly improve cash flow, stabilize their financial position, and create new opportunities for growth. Backed by the U.S. Small Business Administration, SBA refinancing programs are designed to provide tangible benefits to borrowers, ensuring that the new loan improves their financial situation rather than simply replacing one obligation with another.

At its core, refinancing with an SBA loan involves replacing existing debt with a new loan that offers better terms. These improvements can include lower interest rates, longer repayment periods, reduced monthly payments, or a combination of all three. The goal is to create a more manageable financial structure that aligns with the borrower's current business performance and future objectives. Unlike conventional refinancing, which often requires strict credit and collateral standards, SBA refinancing is more flexible and considers the overall strength of the business.

One of the most common reasons for refinancing is high-interest debt. Many businesses rely on short-term loans, lines of credit, or merchant cash advances during their early stages. While these financing options can provide quick access to capital, they often come with high interest rates and aggressive repayment schedules. Over time, these obligations can strain cash flow and limit the business's ability to grow. By refinancing these debts into a long-term SBA loan, borrowers can spread payments over a longer period and reduce the overall cost of borrowing.

Another key reason for refinancing is debt consolidation. Businesses often accumulate multiple loans over time, each with its own terms, rates, and payment schedules. Managing these obligations can become complex and inefficient. SBA refinancing allows borrowers to combine multiple debts into a single loan, simplifying their financial structure and reducing administrative burden. This consolidation not only improves organization but also provides a clearer picture of the business's financial health. The concept of "tangible benefit" is central to SBA refinancing guidelines. Lenders must demonstrate that the new loan provides a clear advantage to the borrower. This could include a reduction in monthly payments, a lower interest rate, improved cash flow, or a more stable repayment structure. This requirement ensures that refinancing is used as a tool for improvement rather than unnecessary debt restructuring.

Cash flow improvement is often the most immediate and impactful benefit of refinancing. By extending the loan term from, for example, 10 years to 25 years, borrowers can significantly reduce their monthly payments. This reduction frees up capital that can be reinvested into the business, used to build reserves, or allocated toward expansion initiatives. Improved cash flow also enhances the business's ability to weather economic fluctuations and maintain stability during challenging periods.

SBA 7(a) loans are commonly used for refinancing because of their flexibility. They can be used to refinance a wide range of debts, including commercial mortgages, business loans, and even certain types of unsecured debt. The ability to include working capital in the refinancing structure further enhances the borrower's financial position, providing additional liquidity for operations and growth.

SBA 504 loans can also be used for refinancing, particularly when the debt being refinanced is tied to fixed assets such as real estate or equipment. The 504 refinance program allows borrowers to access long-term, fixed-rate financing, providing stability and predictability. This is especially valuable in rising interest rate environments, where locking in a fixed rate can protect the business from future increases.

Another important aspect of refinancing is equity utilization. As property values increase and loan balances decrease, borrowers build equity in their real estate. SBA refinancing programs may allow borrowers to access a portion of this equity, converting it into usable capital. This capital can be used for business expansion, improvements, or other strategic initiatives, effectively turning a passive asset into an active financial resource.

Prepayment penalties are a critical consideration when refinancing. Many existing loans include penalties for early payoff, which can impact the overall cost of refinancing. Borrowers must carefully evaluate these costs and compare them to the long-term savings generated by the new loan. In many cases, the benefits of lower payments and improved cash flow outweigh the cost of the penalty, but this analysis must be done carefully.

Timing plays a significant role in refinancing decisions. Interest rate trends, business performance, and market conditions all influence the optimal timing for refinancing. Borrowers should aim to refinance when their business is performing well, as this strengthens their application and increases the likelihood of favorable terms. Waiting until financial difficulties arise can limit options and reduce the effectiveness of refinancing.

Risk management is also an essential component of refinancing strategy. While extending loan terms can improve cash flow, it may also increase the total interest paid over the life of the loan. Borrowers must balance short-term benefits with long-term costs, ensuring that the refinancing structure aligns with their overall financial goals. In some cases, making additional principal payments can offset the increased interest and accelerate loan payoff.

Another strategic advantage of SBA refinancing is the ability to reposition the business for future opportunities. By improving cash flow and simplifying debt structure, borrowers can strengthen their financial profile, making it easier to qualify for additional financing in the future. This can be particularly valuable for businesses planning to expand, acquire additional properties, or invest in new ventures.

As you move through this chapter, it becomes clear that refinancing with SBA mortgage loans is not just about reducing payments—it is about transforming the financial structure of your business. It provides an opportunity to reset, optimize, and position yourself for long-term success. By understanding how to evaluate refinancing opportunities and structure them effectively, you can unlock significant value and create a more stable and scalable business.

This chapter provides the framework for using SBA refinancing strategically. As you continue through this series, you will learn how to integrate refinancing into broader financial strategies and how to use it as a tool for growth, stability, and wealth creation.

Real-Life Math Example: SBA Refinancing Scenario

Let's walk through a detailed real-life scenario to illustrate how SBA refinancing works in practice.

Imagine a business owner named Kevin who owns a distribution company. He currently has two loans: a commercial mortgage with a balance of $800,000 at an interest rate of 8% with 15 years remaining, and a business loan with a balance of $200,000 at an interest rate of 10% with 5 years remaining.

Kevin's current monthly payments are approximately $7,650 for the mortgage and $4,250 for the business loan, resulting in a total monthly payment of $11,900, or $142,800 annually. These high payments are putting pressure on his cash flow and limiting his ability to invest in growth.

Kevin decides to refinance both loans into a single SBA 7(a) loan. The new loan amount is $1,000,000, structured over 25 years at an interest rate of 7%. His new monthly payment is approximately $7,065, or $84,780 annually.

This refinancing reduces Kevin's annual debt service from $142,800 to $84,780, resulting in a savings of $58,020 per year. This significant reduction in payments immediately improves his cash flow and provides additional capital for business operations.

Kevin's business generates $300,000 in annual net operating income. Before refinancing, his debt service coverage ratio (DSCR) was approximately 2.10 ($300,000 divided by $142,800). After refinancing, his DSCR improves to approximately 3.54 ($300,000 divided by $84,780), indicating a much stronger financial position.

Kevin also uses $50,000 in additional loan proceeds for working capital, allowing him to invest in inventory and expand his distribution network. This investment increases his annual net income to $340,000 within the first year. Now, Kevin's DSCR is approximately 4.01 ($340,000 divided by $84,780), further strengthening his financial stability and positioning him for future growth.

Let's analyze the long-term impact. While Kevin's new loan term is longer, resulting in more total interest over time, the improved cash flow allows him to make additional principal payments of $1,500 per month. This reduces the effective loan term and offsets the additional interest cost.

Over 10 years, Kevin will have significantly reduced his loan balance while also benefiting from improved cash flow and business growth. If his property appreciates at 3% annually, the value of his real estate could increase substantially, further enhancing his net worth.

This example demonstrates how SBA refinancing can transform a business's financial structure. By consolidating debt, reducing payments, and improving cash flow, Kevin is able to stabilize his operations and create new opportunities for growth.

The numbers clearly illustrate the power of SBA refinancing. It is not just about lowering payments—it is about creating a stronger, more flexible financial foundation that supports long-term success.

Chapter 8

Using SBA Mortgage Loans for Construction and Expansion

SBA commercial mortgage loans are not only powerful tools for acquiring existing properties or refinancing debt, but they also provide a strategic pathway for construction, renovation, and expansion. For business owners who have outgrown their current space or require a customized facility to support operations, SBA financing offers a structured and accessible way to build or improve commercial real estate. Backed by the U.S. Small Business Administration, these programs are designed to support long-term business growth by enabling borrowers to create environments that align with their operational needs and future vision.

Construction and expansion financing under SBA programs typically falls under two primary categories: SBA 7(a) loans and SBA 504 loans. Each program offers unique advantages depending on the scope and nature of the project. The SBA 7(a) program provides flexibility, allowing borrowers to include construction costs, working capital, equipment, and other business expenses within a single loan. This makes it ideal for projects that involve both real estate development and operational expansion. On the other hand, the SBA 504 program is specifically tailored for fixed assets, offering long-term, fixed-rate financing for construction and major renovations.

One of the most important aspects of SBA construction financing is the concept of phased funding. Unlike traditional loans where funds are disbursed in a lump sum, construction loans are typically released in stages, known as draws. These draws are tied to the progress of the project, ensuring that funds are used appropriately and that the construction is completed according to plan. This structure provides a level of oversight and accountability that protects both the borrower and the lender.

During the construction phase, borrowers may be required to make interest-only payments on the funds that have been disbursed. This helps reduce the financial burden while the property is not yet generating income. Once construction is complete, the loan transitions into a fully amortizing structure with principal and interest payments over a long-term period, typically up to 25 years. This transition marks the point at which the property begins to contribute to the business's operations and financial performance.

Planning is a critical component of successful construction and expansion projects. Borrowers must develop detailed plans that include architectural designs, cost estimates, timelines, and contractor agreements. Lenders will review these plans carefully to ensure that the project is feasible and aligns with the borrower's business objectives. A well-prepared plan not only improves approval chances but also helps ensure that the project is completed on time and within budget.

Cost management is another key factor in construction financing. Projects often include a variety of expenses, such as land acquisition, site preparation, building materials, labor, permits, and contingency reserves. SBA loans allow many of these costs to be included in the financing, reducing the need for additional capital. However, borrowers must be prepared to manage these costs effectively and account for potential overruns.

One of the most significant advantages of SBA construction financing is the ability to create a customized space that enhances business operations. Unlike existing properties, which may require compromises or adjustments, a new construction project can be designed specifically to meet the needs of the business. This can improve efficiency, increase capacity, and create a better experience for customers and employees. Over time, these improvements can translate into increased revenue and profitability. Expansion projects also provide opportunities for growth and diversification. For example, a business may add new services, increase production capacity, or expand into new markets. SBA financing supports these initiatives by providing the capital needed to execute them effectively. By aligning the physical space with the business strategy, borrowers can create a strong foundation for long-term success.

Another important consideration is the potential for increased property value. New construction and renovations often result in properties that are more valuable than their original cost. This creates immediate equity for the borrower and enhances the overall return on investment. Combined with long-term appreciation, this can significantly increase the borrower's net worth over time.

However, construction and expansion projects also come with risks that must be carefully managed. Delays, cost overruns, and unforeseen challenges can impact the timeline and budget. Borrowers must work with experienced contractors, maintain clear communication, and monitor progress closely to mitigate these risks. SBA lenders also play a role in this process by conducting inspections and ensuring that funds are disbursed appropriately.

The owner-occupancy requirement remains a key factor in SBA construction financing. Borrowers must plan to occupy at least 60% of the property initially, with the intention of increasing occupancy over time. This requirement ensures that the project supports the borrower's business operations while still allowing for potential rental income from unused space.

Cash flow analysis is particularly important in construction projects, as the property may not generate income during the build phase. Borrowers must demonstrate that they have sufficient resources to cover expenses during this period and that the completed project will generate enough income to support the loan. This often involves detailed financial projections and contingency planning.

Another strategic advantage of SBA construction financing is the ability to lock in long-term financing from the beginning. Unlike traditional construction loans that require refinancing after completion, SBA loans can be structured as permanent financing from day one. This eliminates the uncertainty associated with future interest rates and refinancing conditions, providing greater stability and predictability.

As you move through this chapter, it becomes clear that SBA construction and expansion financing is not just about building a property—it is about building a future. It allows business owners to create spaces that support growth, improve efficiency, and enhance profitability. By understanding how to plan, structure, and execute these projects, borrowers can leverage SBA financing to achieve their long-term goals.

This chapter provides a comprehensive overview of how SBA loans can be used for construction and expansion. As you continue through this series, you will learn how to integrate these strategies into broader financial plans and how to use them to create sustainable growth and long-term success.

Real-Life Math Example: SBA Construction and Expansion Scenario

Let's walk through a detailed real-life scenario to illustrate how SBA construction financing works in practice.

Imagine a business owner named Daniel who operates a growing medical clinic. His business generates $450,000 in annual net operating income, and he currently leases a facility for $12,000 per month, or $144,000 annually. Due to increasing demand, Daniel decides to build a new, larger facility that will allow him to expand services and increase patient capacity.

The total project cost is $2,500,000, which includes land acquisition, construction, permits, and equipment. Daniel uses an SBA 504 loan with a 10% down payment of $250,000. The financing structure includes $1,250,000 from a bank (50%) and $1,000,000 from a CDC (40%).

During the 12-month construction period, Daniel makes interest-only payments on the funds that have been disbursed. Assuming an average balance of $1,500,000 during construction at an interest rate of 6.5%, his monthly interest payment is approximately $8,125, or $97,500 annually. This is lower than his current rent, allowing him to manage costs during the build phase.

Once construction is complete, the loan transitions into full amortization. The bank portion of $1,250,000 results in a monthly payment of approximately $8,600, while the CDC portion of $1,000,000 results in a monthly payment of approximately $6,100. Daniel's total monthly payment is approximately $14,700, or $176,400 annually.

At first glance, this is higher than his previous rent. However, Daniel's expanded facility allows him to increase revenue significantly. Within the first year, his net operating income grows from $450,000 to $600,000 due to increased patient volume and additional services.

Now let's calculate Daniel's DSCR. His annual debt service is $176,400. With a net income of $600,000, his DSCR is approximately 3.40, which is well above the minimum requirement. Daniel also leases out a small portion of the building to a physical therapy provider, generating $4,000 per month, or $48,000 annually. This reduces his effective annual cost from $176,400 to $128,400, which is lower than his previous rent when adjusted for increased revenue.

Over time, Daniel's financial position continues to improve. Assuming a 3% annual appreciation rate, the $2,500,000 property could be worth approximately $3,357,000 after 10 years. Combined with principal reduction, Daniel could build over $1,000,000 in equity.

Let's break down the numbers further. After accounting for rental income, Daniel's effective annual cost is $128,400. With a net income of $600,000, he has $471,600 remaining before taxes and reinvestment. This strong cash flow allows him to expand further, hire additional staff, and invest in new technology.

If Daniel continues to grow his business and increase revenue, his financial position will strengthen even further. He may also have opportunities to refinance or expand again in the future, leveraging the equity and stability created by this project.

This example demonstrates how SBA construction financing can be used to build and expand a business while improving financial performance and creating long-term wealth. By leveraging structured financing and strategic planning, borrowers can turn their vision into reality and achieve sustainable growth.

Chapter 9

SBA Mortgage Loan Requirements, Rates, and Loan Structures

Understanding SBA mortgage loan requirements, interest rates, and loan structures is essential for any borrower who wants to successfully navigate the approval process and optimize their financing strategy. While SBA loans offer flexibility and accessibility, they are still governed by a detailed framework that determines how loans are structured, priced, and approved. By mastering these elements, borrowers can position themselves more effectively, negotiate better terms, and make informed decisions that support long-term financial success. Backed by the U.S. Small Business Administration, SBA mortgage programs are designed to balance borrower accessibility with lender risk management, creating a system that benefits both parties.

At the foundation of SBA loan requirements is borrower eligibility, which includes factors such as business type, size, and purpose. As discussed in earlier chapters, borrowers must operate a for-profit business, meet SBA size standards, and demonstrate a clear business purpose for the loan. However, beyond these basic requirements, lenders evaluate a range of additional criteria, including creditworthiness, cash flow, collateral, and management experience. These factors collectively determine the borrower's risk profile and influence the terms of the loan.

Interest rates are one of the most important components of SBA loan structures. SBA 7(a) loans typically have variable interest rates that are tied to a benchmark such as the prime rate. Lenders can add a margin on top of this benchmark, which is capped by SBA guidelines. For example, a loan might be priced at the prime rate plus 2.75%, depending on the loan size and term. This structure allows rates to adjust over time, which can be beneficial in declining rate environments but may increase payments if rates rise.

In contrast, SBA 504 loans offer a combination of fixed and variable rates. The CDC portion of the loan is typically fixed for the entire term, providing long-term stability, while the bank portion may be fixed or variable depending on the lender. This hybrid structure allows borrowers to benefit from both stability and flexibility, making it an attractive option for long-term real estate financing.

Loan terms are another critical aspect of SBA mortgage structures. Real estate loans can extend up to 25 years, significantly reducing monthly payments compared to shorter-term financing. Equipment loans typically have terms of 10 years, while working capital loans may have shorter durations. The ability to extend repayment over a long period improves cash flow and allows businesses to allocate resources more effectively.

Amortization is closely tied to loan terms and determines how payments are applied over time. In a fully amortizing loan, each payment includes both principal and interest, gradually reducing the loan balance. SBA loans are typically fully amortizing, which means borrowers do not face balloon payments at the end of the term. This provides greater predictability and reduces refinancing risk.

Fees are another important consideration in SBA loan structures. These can include guarantee fees, packaging fees, closing costs, and ongoing servicing fees. The SBA guarantee fee is typically based on the loan amount and the portion guaranteed by the SBA. While these fees may increase the upfront cost of the loan, they are often offset by the favorable terms and lower down payment requirements.

Collateral requirements vary depending on the loan and borrower profile. While SBA loans are primarily cash flow-based, lenders will still seek to secure the loan with available assets. This includes the commercial property being financed and, in some cases, additional personal or business assets. However, a lack of sufficient collateral does not automatically disqualify a borrower, as the SBA guarantee helps mitigate lender risk.

Loan structure flexibility is one of the defining features of SBA financing. Borrowers can structure loans to include multiple components, such as real estate, business acquisition, equipment, and working capital. This flexibility allows for customized solutions that align with the borrower's specific needs and goals. For example, a borrower purchasing a business with real estate can include all related costs in a single SBA 7(a) loan, simplifying the transaction and reducing complexity.

Another key element of SBA loan structures is the concept of leverage. With down payments as low as 10%, borrowers can control large assets with relatively small upfront investments. This leverage can amplify returns but must be managed carefully to avoid excessive risk. Maintaining a strong DSCR and sufficient reserves is essential to ensuring that the loan remains sustainable over time.

Rate negotiation is an often-overlooked aspect of SBA financing. While SBA guidelines set maximum allowable rates, lenders may offer lower rates depending on the borrower's profile and market conditions. Borrowers with strong credit, stable cash flow, and significant experience may be able to negotiate more favorable terms, including reduced margins or fees.

Prepayment terms also play a role in loan structure. SBA 7(a) loans with terms of 15 years or longer typically include prepayment penalties during the first three years, while SBA 504 loans may have declining prepayment penalties over a longer period. Understanding these terms is important for borrowers who may plan to refinance or sell the property in the future.

Another important consideration is the impact of interest rates on overall loan cost. Even small changes in interest rates can significantly affect total payments over the life of the loan. Borrowers should evaluate different rate scenarios and consider strategies such as making additional principal payments to reduce interest costs.

Risk assessment is a central component of SBA loan structuring. Lenders evaluate not only the borrower's current financial position but also potential risks related to market conditions, industry trends, and economic factors. A well-structured loan should account for these risks and provide a buffer through strong cash flow and reserves.

As you move through this chapter, it becomes clear that SBA loan requirements, rates, and structures are interconnected elements that must be carefully managed. Understanding how these components work together allows borrowers to make informed decisions, optimize their financing, and position themselves for long-term success.

This chapter provides the framework for evaluating SBA loan options and structuring deals effectively. As you continue through this series, you will build on this knowledge and learn how to apply it in more advanced scenarios, ultimately mastering the art of SBA commercial mortgage financing.

Real-Life Math Example: SBA Loan Structure and Rate Analysis

Let's walk through a detailed real-life scenario to understand how SBA loan requirements, rates, and structures impact financial outcomes.

Imagine a borrower named Michael who wants to purchase a commercial property for $1,800,000. He uses an SBA 7(a) loan with a 10% down payment of $180,000, financing $1,620,000.

The loan is structured over 25 years with a variable interest rate of prime (currently 7.5%) plus 2.5%, resulting in a total rate of 10%. Based on this rate, Michael's monthly payment is approximately $14,700, or $176,400 annually. Michael's business generates $420,000 in annual net operating income. To calculate his DSCR, we divide $420,000 by $176,400, resulting in a ratio of approximately 2.38. This indicates that his business can comfortably support the loan.

Now let's analyze how interest rates affect Michael's payments. If the rate decreases to 9%, his monthly payment drops to approximately $13,600, reducing his annual debt service by $13,200. Conversely, if the rate increases to 11%, his monthly payment rises to approximately $15,900, increasing his annual debt service by $14,400.

These changes demonstrate the importance of understanding rate structures and planning for potential fluctuations. Michael decides to mitigate this risk by making additional principal payments of $1,200 per month, which reduces his loan balance more quickly and lowers total interest paid over time.

Michael also negotiates with his lender to reduce the margin from 2.5% to 2.25%, lowering his initial rate and saving thousands of dollars over the life of the loan. This highlights the importance of rate negotiation and borrower positioning.

Now let's consider fees. Michael pays an SBA guarantee fee of approximately 3% on the guaranteed portion of the loan, which adds to his upfront costs. However, this fee allows him to secure financing with only 10% down, preserving capital for other uses. Over 10 years, assuming a 3% annual appreciation rate, the $1,800,000 property could be worth approximately $2,417,000. Combined with principal reduction, Michael could build over $700,000 in equity.

Let's break down the numbers further. Michael's annual debt service is $176,400, leaving him with $243,600 in remaining income before taxes and reinvestment. This strong cash flow allows him to continue growing his business and exploring additional opportunities.

If Michael leases out a portion of the property for $2,000 per month, or $24,000 annually, his effective debt cost decreases, further improving his financial position.

This example demonstrates how SBA loan requirements, rates, and structures influence the overall financial outcome. By understanding these elements and making strategic decisions, borrowers can optimize their financing and create a strong foundation for long-term success.

The numbers clearly show that SBA loans are not just about access to capital—they are about structuring that capital in a way that maximizes efficiency, stability, and growth.

Chapter 10

Advanced SBA Commercial Mortgage Loan Structuring

As you reach this final chapter of *The SBA Commercial Mortgage Loan Mastery Series*, you are transitioning from foundational knowledge into advanced strategy. At this level, SBA commercial mortgage loans are no longer just tools for financing—they become instruments for optimization, leverage, scalability, and long-term wealth engineering. The true power of SBA financing lies not only in qualifying for a loan, but in how that loan is structured to align with your business model, risk tolerance, and future growth plans. Backed by the U.S. Small Business Administration, these programs provide the framework, but it is the borrower's strategy that determines the outcome.

Advanced structuring begins with understanding how to layer multiple objectives into a single loan. Instead of viewing a transaction as a simple purchase or refinance, experienced borrowers structure deals to accomplish several goals simultaneously. This may include acquiring real estate, funding business expansion, consolidating debt, and preserving liquidity—all within one SBA loan. By combining these elements, borrowers can maximize efficiency and reduce the need for multiple financing sources.

One of the most powerful advanced strategies is optimizing leverage while maintaining strong cash flow. Leverage allows you to control larger assets with less capital, but excessive leverage can create financial strain. The key is to find the balance where the loan enhances your business rather than burdening it. This is achieved by carefully managing the debt service coverage ratio (DSCR), ensuring that the business generates sufficient income to comfortably support the loan. Advanced borrowers often aim for DSCR levels well above the minimum requirement, creating a buffer that protects against economic fluctuations.

Another critical element of advanced structuring is integrating multiple income streams into the deal. For example, an owner-occupied property may include rental income from tenants, revenue from business operations, and potential future income from expansion. By incorporating these income streams into the underwriting analysis, borrowers can strengthen their application and improve loan terms. This approach transforms the property into a multi-dimensional asset that supports both operations and investment growth. Timing and sequencing also play a significant role in advanced SBA loan structuring. Instead of pursuing a single transaction, experienced borrowers plan a series of moves that build upon each other. For example, a borrower may start by acquiring a property with an SBA loan, then use the increased cash flow and equity to refinance or expand into additional properties. This step-by-step approach allows for controlled growth and reduces risk while maximizing long-term returns.

Another advanced strategy involves combining SBA loans with other financing tools. While SBA loans provide a strong foundation, they can be complemented with lines of credit, equipment financing, or private capital to create a more comprehensive financial structure. This hybrid approach allows borrowers to address different needs with the most appropriate financing source, optimizing both cost and flexibility.

Equity management is another key component of advanced structuring. As properties appreciate and loan balances decrease, borrowers build equity that can be leveraged for future investments. SBA refinancing programs may allow borrowers to access this equity, converting it into working capital or funding for expansion. This creates a cycle of growth where each transaction builds upon the previous one, accelerating wealth creation over time.

Risk mitigation is essential when structuring complex deals. Advanced borrowers anticipate potential challenges and build safeguards into their financing structure. This may include maintaining cash reserves, diversifying income streams, and avoiding over-reliance on a single source of revenue. By proactively managing risk, borrowers can ensure that their financing remains sustainable even in changing market conditions.

Another important aspect of advanced structuring is negotiating terms with lenders. While SBA guidelines set certain parameters, there is still room for negotiation in areas such as interest rates, fees, and repayment terms. Borrowers with strong financial profiles and well-structured deals are often able to secure more favorable terms, reducing the overall cost of the loan and improving long-term returns.

Tax strategy also plays a role in advanced SBA loan structuring. Interest payments, depreciation, and other expenses may provide tax benefits that enhance cash flow and reduce overall costs. Working with financial professionals to integrate tax planning into your financing strategy can significantly improve the efficiency of your investments.

Portfolio thinking is another hallmark of advanced SBA loan strategy. Instead of focusing on individual transactions, borrowers consider how each deal fits into a larger portfolio of assets. This includes evaluating diversification, cash flow stability, and long-term growth potential. By building a portfolio of owner-occupied and income-generating properties, borrowers can create a balanced and resilient financial structure.

Exit strategy is equally important. Every loan should be structured with a clear understanding of how it will be managed over time and eventually exited. This may involve refinancing, selling the property, or transitioning it into a different use. Having a defined exit strategy ensures that the loan remains aligned with your long-term goals and provides flexibility as circumstances change.

Another advanced concept is value creation through repositioning. Borrowers can acquire properties that are underutilized or in need of improvement, then enhance their value through renovations, operational changes, or tenant improvements. SBA financing can support these initiatives, allowing borrowers to increase property value and generate higher returns.

As you integrate these strategies, it becomes clear that advanced SBA loan structuring is both an art and a science. It requires a deep understanding of financial principles, market dynamics, and business operations, as well as the ability to think strategically and adapt to changing conditions. The most successful borrowers are those who approach financing as a long-term strategy rather than a one-time transaction.

This chapter represents the culmination of everything you have learned in this series. From understanding basic loan programs to mastering advanced structuring techniques, you now have the knowledge to navigate SBA commercial mortgage financing with confidence. The next step is to apply this knowledge, analyze opportunities, and take action.

By leveraging SBA loans strategically, you can create a powerful foundation for business growth, real estate ownership, and long-term wealth. The tools are available, the strategies are proven, and the opportunities are abundant. The question is how you will use them.

Real-Life Math Example: Advanced SBA Loan Structuring Scenario

Let's walk through a comprehensive real-life scenario that demonstrates advanced SBA loan structuring in action.

Imagine an experienced entrepreneur named Jonathan who owns a successful logistics company generating $500,000 in annual net operating income. Jonathan wants to acquire a new commercial property for $2,200,000, consolidate existing debt of $300,000, and include $100,000 in working capital—all within a single SBA 7(a) loan. The total loan amount is $2,600,000. Jonathan provides a 10% down payment of $260,000, financing $2,340,000 over 25 years at an interest rate of 7.25%. His monthly payment is approximately $16,000, or $192,000 annually.

Now let's analyze the structure. Jonathan's business generates $500,000 in net operating income. His DSCR is calculated as $500,000 divided by $192,000, which equals approximately 2.60. This strong ratio indicates that the business can comfortably support the loan.

Jonathan also leases out 30% of the property, generating $4,500 per month, or $54,000 annually. This reduces his effective annual debt cost from $192,000 to $138,000.

Now let's recalculate his effective DSCR using the rental-adjusted cost. $500,000 divided by $138,000 equals approximately 3.62, further strengthening his financial position.

Jonathan uses the $100,000 in working capital to expand his operations, increasing his annual net income to $600,000 within two years. At this level, his DSCR improves even further, providing additional financial flexibility.

Over time, Jonathan implements an aggressive principal reduction strategy, paying an additional $2,000 per month toward the loan. This reduces the loan balance more quickly and lowers total interest paid.

Let's analyze the long-term impact. Assuming a 3% annual appreciation rate, the $2,200,000 property could be worth approximately $2,955,000 after 10 years. Combined with principal reduction, Jonathan could build over $1,000,000 in equity.

Additionally, Jonathan uses improved cash flow to acquire a second property after five years, leveraging his increased equity and strong financial profile. This creates a portfolio effect, where each asset contributes to overall growth and stability.

Breaking down the numbers further, Jonathan's adjusted annual cost after rental income is $138,000. With a net income of $600,000, he has $462,000 remaining before taxes and reinvestment. This strong cash flow allows him to continue expanding and diversifying his business.

If interest rates decrease, Jonathan may choose to refinance, further reducing his costs and improving his financial position. Alternatively, he may hold the property long-term, benefiting from appreciation and equity growth.

This example illustrates how advanced SBA loan structuring can be used to achieve multiple objectives simultaneously: acquiring property, consolidating debt, increasing income, and building long-term wealth. By understanding and applying these strategies, borrowers can transform SBA financing into a powerful engine for growth and success.

The numbers clearly demonstrate that SBA loans, when structured strategically, are not just financial tools—they are pathways to financial independence, scalability, and long-term prosperity.

Chapter 11

Building a Scalable SBA Commercial Mortgage Strategy for Long-Term Wealth

At this stage in your journey through SBA commercial mortgage financing, you have developed a deep understanding of loan programs, eligibility requirements, structuring techniques, and strategic applications. Now, the focus shifts from individual transactions to building a scalable system that allows you to repeatedly acquire, optimize, and expand commercial real estate and business assets over time. This is where SBA financing evolves from a one-time opportunity into a long-term wealth-building strategy. Supported by programs backed by the U.S. Small Business Administration, this system allows disciplined borrowers to create compounding growth through structured execution.

The first principle of scalability is repeatability. A scalable SBA strategy is not dependent on a single deal or a unique opportunity—it is built on a repeatable process that can be applied across multiple transactions. This process includes identifying opportunities, analyzing cash flow, structuring financing, executing the acquisition, and optimizing the asset.

By refining this process, borrowers can move more efficiently from one deal to the next, reducing friction and increasing momentum.

The second principle is cash flow dominance. While equity and appreciation are important, sustainable growth is driven by consistent and reliable cash flow. Each property or business acquired through SBA financing should contribute positively to overall income, either directly through operations or indirectly through rental income. Strong cash flow not only supports loan repayment but also provides the capital needed to pursue additional opportunities.

Another key element of scalability is capital preservation. SBA loans already provide an advantage with lower down payments, typically around 10%, but advanced borrowers take this further by managing their capital strategically. Instead of deploying all available funds into a single transaction, they maintain reserves and allocate capital across multiple opportunities. This approach reduces risk and ensures that they are always positioned to act when new opportunities arise.

Portfolio diversification is another critical factor in building a scalable strategy. Rather than concentrating all investments in a single property or industry, borrowers can spread their investments across different asset types, locations, and business models. This diversification reduces risk and creates multiple streams of income, enhancing overall stability.

Sequencing is where true strategy comes into play. Instead of approaching each deal independently, advanced borrowers plan their transactions in a sequence that builds upon previous successes. For example, the first SBA loan may be used to acquire an owner-occupied property that generates strong cash flow. Over time, the borrower builds equity and improves financial performance, making it easier to qualify for additional financing. This creates a cycle of growth where each step strengthens the next.

Refinancing plays a crucial role in scalability. As properties appreciate and loan balances decrease, borrowers can refinance to access equity, reduce payments, or restructure debt. This allows them to recycle capital and reinvest it into new opportunities. SBA refinancing programs provide a structured way to achieve this while maintaining favorable terms.

Another important aspect is operational efficiency. As a portfolio grows, managing multiple properties and businesses becomes more complex. Borrowers must implement systems and processes that allow them to operate efficiently, whether through automation, delegation, or professional management. Efficient operations ensure that growth does not lead to increased risk or reduced performance.

Risk management becomes even more critical at scale. While SBA financing provides a strong foundation, borrowers must actively manage risk by maintaining reserves, monitoring performance, and adapting to market conditions. This includes preparing for economic downturns, changes in interest rates, and shifts in demand. A resilient strategy is one that can withstand challenges while continuing to grow.

Another advanced concept is leveraging relationships. Building strong relationships with lenders, brokers, contractors, and advisors can significantly enhance your ability to execute deals. Experienced lenders, in particular, can provide valuable insights, faster approvals, and more favorable terms. These relationships become increasingly valuable as you scale your portfolio.

Tax strategy also becomes more impactful as your portfolio grows. Depreciation, interest deductions, and other tax benefits can significantly improve cash flow and overall returns. Working with tax professionals to optimize your strategy ensures that you are maximizing these benefits while remaining compliant with regulations.

Exit strategies must also be integrated into your scalable system. Each property or loan should have a clear plan for the future, whether that involves refinancing, selling, or transitioning to a different use. Having defined exit strategies provides flexibility and ensures that your investments remain aligned with your long-term goals.

As you continue to scale, mindset becomes a defining factor. Successful borrowers think in terms of systems, not transactions. They focus on long-term growth rather than short-term gains, and they approach each decision with a strategic perspective. This mindset allows them to navigate challenges, identify opportunities, and build sustainable wealth over time.

Ultimately, building a scalable SBA commercial mortgage strategy is about creating a system that works for you. It is about using financing as a tool to acquire assets, generate income, and build equity in a structured and repeatable way. By combining the principles outlined in this chapter with the knowledge gained throughout this series, you can create a powerful framework for long-term success.

This chapter represents the evolution from learning to execution. You now have the tools, the strategies, and the understanding needed to take action. The next step is to apply what you have learned, refine your approach, and build a portfolio that supports your financial goals and aspirations.

Real-Life Math Example: Scalable SBA Portfolio Strategy

Let's walk through a real-life scenario that demonstrates how a borrower can scale using SBA financing over time.

Imagine an entrepreneur named Alex who starts with a business generating $350,000 in annual net operating income. Alex uses an SBA 7(a) loan to purchase an owner-occupied property for $1,500,000 with a 10% down payment of $150,000. The loan amount is $1,350,000 at 7% over 25 years, resulting in an annual debt service of approximately $114,000.

Alex leases out 30% of the property, generating $36,000 annually in rental income. This reduces the effective annual cost to $78,000. With a net income of $350,000, Alex has $272,000 remaining before taxes and reinvestment.

After three years, Alex's business grows, increasing net income to $450,000. The property also appreciates to approximately $1,640,000. Alex refinances the loan, reducing the interest rate and accessing $200,000 in equity.

Alex uses this $200,000 as a down payment on a second property valued at $2,000,000, again using an SBA loan structure. The new loan has an annual debt service of

$150,000, but the property generates $60,000 in rental income, reducing the effective cost. Now Alex has two properties. Combined, they generate strong cash flow and significant equity growth. Alex's total net income increases to $600,000, and the combined debt service remains manageable due to strong DSCR ratios.

Over the next five years, both properties appreciate at 3% annually. The first property grows to approximately $1,900,000, and the second to approximately $2,300,000. Combined with principal reduction, Alex builds over $1,000,000 in equity.

Alex continues this process, using refinancing and cash flow to acquire additional properties. By year 10, Alex owns four properties with a combined value of over $8,000,000 and generates over $800,000 in annual net income.

Let's break down the numbers further. Alex's total annual debt service across all properties is approximately $400,000, while total income exceeds $800,000. This results in a DSCR of 2.0, indicating a strong and sustainable financial position.

Additionally, rental income across the portfolio exceeds $200,000 annually, providing a diversified income stream that enhances stability.

This example demonstrates how SBA financing can be used to build a scalable portfolio over time. By starting with one property, optimizing cash flow, and reinvesting strategically, Alex is able to create a compounding growth effect that leads to significant wealth creation.

The key takeaway is that SBA loans are not just for single transactions—they are tools for building systems. When used strategically, they can support a long-term plan that transforms income into assets, assets into equity, and equity into opportunity.

This is the ultimate goal of SBA commercial mortgage mastery: creating a system that allows you to grow, scale, and achieve financial independence through structured and strategic execution.

Chapter 12

The Ultimate SBA Commercial Mortgage Blueprint — From First Deal to Financial Freedom

As you reach the final chapter of this series, everything comes together into a single, powerful framework. You are no longer just learning about SBA commercial mortgage loans—you are now positioned to implement a complete system that can take you from your first deal to long-term financial independence. The journey you have taken through this series has covered fundamentals, qualification, acquisition, refinancing, construction, and advanced structuring. Now, the focus is on execution at the highest level—creating a repeatable, scalable blueprint that transforms knowledge into results. Supported by programs backed by the U.S. Small Business Administration, this blueprint is designed to help you build, grow, and sustain a portfolio that generates income, equity, and opportunity over time.

The first step in this blueprint is clarity of vision. Before entering into any transaction, you must define your long-term goals. Are you looking to replace your income, build a portfolio, scale a business, or create generational wealth? Your answer will determine how you structure your deals, how aggressively you grow, and how you manage risk. Without a clear vision, it is easy to make decisions that are misaligned with your objectives. With clarity, every action becomes intentional and strategic.

The second step is building your foundation. This includes strengthening your financial profile, improving your credit, organizing your documentation, and establishing relationships with lenders and advisors. A strong foundation increases your chances of approval and allows you to move quickly when opportunities arise. It also positions you to negotiate better terms and access larger amounts of capital over time.

The third step is identifying the right opportunities. Not all deals are created equal, and successful borrowers develop the ability to evaluate opportunities quickly and accurately. This involves analyzing cash flow, understanding market conditions, and assessing the potential for growth and value creation. The goal is to find deals that align with your strategy and provide a strong balance of income and long-term appreciation.

The fourth step is structuring the deal effectively. This is where the knowledge you have gained throughout this series becomes critical. You must determine the appropriate loan program, optimize leverage, include necessary components such as working capital, and ensure that the deal meets SBA requirements. A well-structured deal not only improves approval chances but also sets the stage for long-term success.

Execution is the fifth step. This involves navigating the loan process, coordinating with lenders, completing due diligence, and closing the transaction. Attention to detail is essential during this phase, as small mistakes can lead to delays or complications. Working with experienced professionals can help streamline the process and ensure a smooth closing.

The sixth step is optimization. Once the deal is closed, the focus shifts to maximizing performance. This may involve increasing revenue, reducing expenses, improving operations, or enhancing the property. The goal is to strengthen cash flow and build equity as quickly as possible. Optimization is an ongoing process that continues throughout the life of the investment.

The seventh step is leverage and expansion. As your financial position improves, you can begin to use your success to fuel additional growth. This may involve refinancing to access equity, acquiring additional properties, or expanding your business operations. Each step builds on the previous one, creating a compounding effect that accelerates your progress.

The eighth step is systemization. As your portfolio grows, you must develop systems and processes that allow you to manage multiple assets efficiently. This includes financial tracking, property management, and operational workflows. Systemization ensures that growth does not lead to chaos and that your business remains scalable.

The ninth step is risk management. Every investment carries risk, and successful borrowers proactively manage these risks. This includes maintaining reserves, diversifying income streams, and planning for potential challenges. A strong risk management strategy ensures that your portfolio remains stable even in changing market conditions.

The tenth step is long-term strategy and exit planning. Each deal should have a clear purpose within your overall portfolio. This may include holding for long-term income, refinancing for better terms, or selling to capture gains. Having a defined strategy allows you to make decisions with confidence and adapt to changing circumstances.

As you integrate these steps, you begin to see how they form a cohesive blueprint. This is not about isolated transactions—it is about building a system that generates consistent results over time. Each step reinforces the others, creating a cycle of growth, stability, and opportunity.

Mindset is the final and perhaps most important element of this blueprint. Success in SBA commercial mortgage financing requires discipline, patience, and strategic thinking. It requires the ability to see opportunities where others see obstacles and to take calculated risks that align with your goals. By maintaining the right mindset, you can navigate challenges and continue moving forward.

This chapter represents the culmination of everything you have learned. It is your guide to turning knowledge into action and action into results. The blueprint is clear, the tools are available, and the opportunity is in front of you.

The next step is yours.

Real-Life Math Example: From First Deal to Financial Freedom

Let's walk through a comprehensive real-life scenario that demonstrates how this blueprint works in practice.

Imagine an entrepreneur named Sofia who starts with a consulting business generating $300,000 in annual net operating income. She purchases her first property for $1,200,000 using an SBA loan with a 10% down payment of $120,000. The loan amount is $1,080,000 at 7% over 25 years, resulting in an annual debt service of approximately $91,000.

Sofia leases out 25% of the property, generating $24,000 annually. This reduces her effective cost to $67,000. With a net income of $300,000, she has $233,000 remaining before taxes and reinvestment.

Over three years, Sofia grows her business, increasing net income to $400,000. The property appreciates to approximately $1,310,000. She refinances, accessing $150,000 in equity.

Sofia uses this $150,000 as a down payment on a second property valued at $1,800,000. The new loan has an annual debt service of $140,000, but the property generates $50,000 in rental income, reducing the effective cost.

Now Sofia owns two properties and generates strong cash flow. Her total income increases to $550,000, and her combined debt service remains manageable.

Over the next five years, both properties appreciate at 3% annually. The first property grows to approximately $1,520,000, and the second to approximately $2,085,000. Combined with principal reduction, Sofia builds over $800,000 in equity.

Sofia continues this process, acquiring a third property using the equity and cash flow generated from her first two investments. By year 10, she owns three properties with a combined value of over $5,000,000 and generates over $700,000 in annual net income. Let's break down the numbers further. Sofia's total annual debt service is approximately $300,000, while her income exceeds $700,000. This results in a DSCR of approximately 2.33, indicating a strong and sustainable financial position.

Additionally, her rental income exceeds $120,000 annually, providing diversification and stability.

As Sofia continues to grow, she reaches a point where her passive income from rental properties and business operations exceeds her living expenses. At this stage, she has achieved financial independence.

This example demonstrates how SBA financing can be used to build wealth step by step. By starting with one deal, optimizing performance, and reinvesting strategically, Sofia creates a compounding effect that leads to long-term success.

The blueprint is simple but powerful: acquire, optimize, leverage, and repeat.

When executed consistently, this strategy can transform your financial future and create opportunities that extend far beyond a single transaction.

Chapter 13

Mastering SBA Commercial Mortgage Execution — From Application to Closing and Beyond

At this stage in your journey, you understand the strategies, structures, and opportunities that SBA commercial mortgage financing provides. However, knowledge alone does not create results—execution does. The difference between borrowers who succeed and those who struggle often comes down to how well they navigate the process from application to closing and how effectively they manage the loan afterward. In this chapter, we focus on mastering execution at every stage, turning your understanding into consistent, repeatable outcomes. Supported by programs backed by the U.S. Small Business Administration, the process is structured, but your preparation and approach determine how smoothly it unfolds.

The first stage of execution is pre-application preparation. This is where most successful borrowers gain their advantage. Before you ever submit a loan application, you should have your financial documents organized, your business story clearly defined, and your strategy fully outlined. This includes personal and business tax returns, profit and loss statements, balance sheets, and projections. It also includes a clear explanation of how the loan will be used and how it will benefit your business. Lenders are not just evaluating numbers—they are evaluating confidence, clarity, and credibility.

The second stage is lender selection. Choosing the right lender is critical to a successful outcome. SBA Preferred Lenders have the authority to approve loans more quickly and often have more experience structuring deals. Working with a lender who understands your industry and your goals can significantly reduce friction in the process. This is not just a transaction—it is a relationship that can support your growth over time.

Once the lender is selected, the application phase begins. This involves submitting your loan package, which includes financial documents, business plans, and details about the property or transaction. Accuracy and completeness are essential. Missing or inconsistent information can delay the process and raise concerns during underwriting. A well-prepared application demonstrates professionalism and reduces the likelihood of additional requests.

The underwriting stage is where the lender evaluates your application in detail. This includes analyzing your credit, cash flow, collateral, and overall risk profile. Underwriters will assess your debt service coverage ratio (DSCR), review your financial history, and evaluate the viability of your business. This stage may involve questions and requests for additional documentation. Responding quickly and clearly is key to maintaining momentum.

One of the most important aspects of underwriting is the narrative you present. Numbers tell part of the story, but context completes it. If there are inconsistencies, gaps, or challenges in your financial history, you must address them proactively. Transparency builds trust, and trust accelerates approval.

The next stage is approval and commitment. Once the lender is satisfied with your application, they issue a commitment letter outlining the terms of the loan. This includes the loan amount, interest rate, repayment terms, and any conditions that must be met before closing. Reviewing this document carefully is essential, as it defines the structure of your financing.

Due diligence follows approval. This includes property appraisals, environmental reports, title searches, and other verifications. These steps ensure that the property and transaction meet all requirements and that there are no hidden risks. While this stage can take time, it is critical for protecting both the borrower and the lender. The closing stage is where everything comes together. Documents are finalized, funds are disbursed, and ownership is transferred. Attention to detail is essential, as errors at this stage can create complications. Working with experienced professionals, such as attorneys and closing agents, can help ensure a smooth process.

However, execution does not end at closing—it evolves into management. Once the loan is in place, your focus shifts to performance. This includes managing cash flow, maintaining the property, and ensuring that your business continues to generate sufficient income to support the loan. Strong post-closing management is what transforms a successful transaction into a long-term success.

Monitoring performance is a critical part of this stage. Regularly reviewing financial statements, tracking key metrics, and adjusting strategies as needed ensures that you remain on track. This proactive approach allows you to identify challenges early and take corrective action before they become significant issues.

Another important aspect of execution is communication. Maintaining open lines of communication with your lender can be beneficial, especially if you plan to pursue additional financing in the future. Lenders value borrowers who are transparent, responsive, and proactive.

Scaling execution is the next level. Once you have successfully completed one SBA loan, you can refine your process and apply it to future transactions. Each deal becomes easier as you gain experience, build relationships, and develop systems. This is where execution becomes a competitive advantage.

Time management also plays a role in execution. SBA loans involve multiple steps and parties, and delays can occur if timelines are not managed effectively. Staying organized, setting clear deadlines, and following up consistently helps keep the process moving forward.

Risk management remains a constant consideration. Even after closing, you must be prepared for changes in market conditions, interest rates, and business performance. Maintaining reserves and staying disciplined ensures that your financing remains sustainable.

As you integrate these principles, execution becomes second nature. You move from reacting to the process to controlling it. You anticipate challenges, prepare solutions, and navigate each stage with confidence.

This chapter represents the bridge between knowledge and action. You now understand not only how SBA loans work, but how to execute them effectively. The ability to execute consistently is what separates successful borrowers from the rest.

Real-Life Math Example: SBA Loan Execution from Start to Finish

Let's walk through a detailed real-life scenario that illustrates the execution process with actual numbers.

Imagine a borrower named Daniel who owns a service business generating $360,000 in annual net operating income. Daniel identifies a commercial property priced at $1,300,000 and decides to pursue an SBA 7(a) loan.

Daniel prepares his financial documents, including tax returns and financial statements, and works with a lender to structure the loan. He provides a 10% down payment of $130,000 and finances $1,170,000 over 25 years at an interest rate of 7%.

His monthly payment is approximately $8,300, resulting in an annual debt service of $99,600.

During underwriting, the lender evaluates Daniel's DSCR. With a net income of $360,000, his DSCR is approximately

3.61 ($360,000 divided by $99,600), which is well above the minimum requirement. This strong ratio supports approval.

Daniel also plans to lease out 20% of the property, generating $2,000 per month, or $24,000 annually. This reduces his effective annual cost from $99,600 to $75,600. After closing, Daniel focuses on optimizing his business. Within two years, he increases his net income to $420,000 through improved operations and marketing.

Now, his DSCR improves further. Using the original debt service of $99,600, his DSCR becomes approximately 4.22. If we consider the rental-adjusted cost of $75,600, his effective DSCR increases to approximately 5.55.

Let's analyze the long-term impact. Over 10 years, Daniel pays down a significant portion of the loan principal. Assuming a 3% annual appreciation rate, the $1,300,000 property grows to approximately $1,747,000.

Combined with principal reduction, Daniel builds over $500,000 in equity.

Daniel also implements a strategy of making additional principal payments of $1,000 per month. This accelerates loan payoff and reduces total interest paid.

Breaking down the numbers further, Daniel's adjusted annual cost after rental income is $75,600. With a net income of $420,000, he has $344,400 remaining before taxes and reinvestment.

This strong cash flow allows him to build reserves, invest in his business, and prepare for future acquisitions. After five years, Daniel uses his improved financial position to acquire a second property, repeating the process and expanding his portfolio.

This example demonstrates how effective execution turns a single SBA loan into a long-term growth strategy. By preparing thoroughly, managing the process efficiently, and optimizing performance after closing, Daniel is able to create a strong financial foundation and position himself for continued success.

The key takeaway is clear: execution is where strategy becomes reality. When done correctly, it transforms opportunities into results and results into long-term wealth.

Chapter 14

SBA Commercial Mortgage Deal Analysis — How to Evaluate, Underwrite, and Choose Winning Deals

At this advanced stage, your success with SBA commercial mortgage financing depends less on access to capital and more on your ability to identify, analyze, and select the right deals. Not every opportunity is worth pursuing, and the difference between average results and exceptional outcomes lies in your ability to evaluate deals with precision. In this chapter, you will learn how to think like an underwriter, analyze opportunities from both a lender's and an investor's perspective, and consistently choose deals that align with your long-term strategy. Supported by frameworks backed by the U.S. Small Business Administration, this approach ensures that your decisions are grounded in both risk management and opportunity maximization.

The foundation of deal analysis begins with understanding cash flow. Cash flow is the engine that drives every successful SBA loan. Without strong and stable income, even the best-structured deal can fail. When evaluating a deal, your first priority is to determine how much net operating income (NOI) the property or business generates and whether that income is sustainable. This involves reviewing financial statements, identifying trends, and understanding the drivers behind the numbers. Consistency is key—lenders prefer stable and predictable income over volatile or uncertain performance.

Once cash flow is established, the next step is calculating the debt service coverage ratio (DSCR). This metric is central to SBA underwriting and serves as a measure of the borrower's ability to repay the loan. A DSCR of 1.25 is typically the minimum requirement, but strong deals often exceed this threshold significantly. As an advanced borrower, you should aim for higher DSCR levels to create a buffer that protects against unforeseen challenges.

The third component of deal analysis is valuation. Understanding how a property or business is valued allows you to determine whether the purchase price is justified. For real estate, this involves analyzing comparable sales, market conditions, and income potential. For businesses, valuation often relies on multiples of earnings, such as EBITDA. A well-priced deal provides immediate value and reduces risk, while an overpriced deal can limit your ability to generate returns.

Another critical factor is leverage. SBA loans allow for high leverage with low down payments, but this must be used strategically. Higher leverage increases potential returns but also amplifies risk. When analyzing a deal, you must consider how much debt the property or business can realistically support without compromising stability. This involves stress-testing your numbers under different scenarios, such as reduced income or increased expenses.

Market analysis is another essential component. A strong deal in a weak market can still underperform, while a good deal in a strong market can exceed expectations. Understanding local economic conditions, demand trends, and growth potential helps you assess the long-term viability of the investment. Factors such as population growth, industry presence, and infrastructure development can significantly impact property value and business performance.

Risk identification is a key part of deal analysis. Every deal carries risks, whether related to market conditions, tenant stability, operational challenges, or financing terms. The goal is not to eliminate risk but to understand and manage it. This involves identifying potential issues, assessing their impact, and developing strategies to mitigate them. A deal with manageable risks and strong upside potential is often more attractive than a seemingly "safe" deal with limited growth.

Another advanced concept is value-add potential. Some of the best deals are not perfect from the start—they require improvements to reach their full potential. This may involve renovating a property, improving operations, increasing rents, or expanding services. SBA financing can support these initiatives, allowing you to create value and increase returns over time. The key is to identify opportunities where your actions can directly influence the outcome.

Exit strategy is also an important consideration during deal analysis. Before entering a deal, you should have a clear understanding of how you plan to exit or reposition the asset. This may involve refinancing, selling, or holding for long-term income. A well-defined exit strategy provides flexibility and ensures that your investment remains aligned with your goals.

Sensitivity analysis is a powerful tool for evaluating deals. This involves testing how changes in key variables—such as interest rates, income, or expenses—affect the overall performance of the deal. By understanding how different scenarios impact your numbers, you can make more informed decisions and prepare for potential challenges.

Another important aspect is aligning the deal with your overall strategy. Not every good deal is the right deal for you. Your decisions should be guided by your long-term goals, whether that involves building a portfolio, scaling a business, or generating passive income. Alignment ensures that each deal contributes to your broader objectives.

As you refine your deal analysis skills, you begin to think like both an investor and a lender. You evaluate opportunities not just based on potential returns but also on risk, sustainability, and strategic fit. This dual perspective allows you to make decisions with confidence and consistency.

Ultimately, mastering deal analysis is about discipline. It requires the ability to say no to deals that do not meet your criteria and the patience to wait for the right opportunities. By applying the principles outlined in this chapter, you can build a portfolio of high-quality assets that support your long-term success.

This chapter represents a critical step in your journey. With strong deal analysis skills, you are no longer dependent on luck or timing—you are in control of your outcomes. The next step is to apply these principles consistently and refine your approach with each deal.

Real-Life Math Example: Deal Analysis and Decision-Making

Let's walk through a detailed real-life scenario to illustrate how deal analysis works in practice. Imagine a borrower named Kevin who is evaluating the purchase of a commercial property priced at $1,600,000. The property generates $180,000 in annual net operating income.

Kevin plans to use an SBA loan with a 10% down payment of $160,000, financing $1,440,000 at an interest rate of 7.25% over 25 years. His annual debt service is approximately $124,000.

To calculate the DSCR, Kevin divides the NOI by the debt service. $180,000 divided by $124,000 equals approximately 1.45. This meets the minimum requirement but is not exceptionally strong.

Kevin then performs a sensitivity analysis. If the NOI decreases by 10%, it drops to $162,000. The new DSCR becomes approximately 1.31, which is still acceptable but closer to the minimum threshold.

Kevin also identifies an opportunity to increase rental income by improving the property and adjusting leases. He estimates that he can increase NOI to $210,000 within two years.

With this increased NOI, the DSCR improves to approximately 1.69, significantly strengthening the deal.

Now let's analyze the long-term potential. Assuming a 3% annual appreciation rate, the property could be worth approximately $2,150,000 after 10 years. Combined with principal reduction, Kevin could build over $700,000 in equity.

Kevin also considers the impact of additional principal payments. By paying an extra $1,000 per month, he reduces the loan balance more quickly and lowers total interest paid.

Let's break down the numbers further. After debt service of $124,000, Kevin has $56,000 in annual cash flow at the current NOI of $180,000. If NOI increases to $210,000, his cash flow rises to $86,000.

Kevin compares this deal to another opportunity with a higher DSCR but lower growth potential. After analyzing both options, he chooses the first deal because of its value-add potential and long-term upside.

This example demonstrates how deal analysis involves more than just current numbers—it requires evaluating potential, risk, and alignment with your strategy.

By applying these principles, Kevin is able to make an informed decision that supports his long-term goals and positions him for growth.

The key takeaway is that successful SBA borrowers do not just take deals—they choose them carefully, analyze them thoroughly, and execute them strategically.

Chapter 15

Creating Generational Wealth with SBA Commercial Mortgage Loans

As you arrive at this final chapter, the focus shifts from transactions, strategies, and execution to the ultimate objective behind all of it—creating lasting, generational wealth. SBA commercial mortgage financing is not just a tool for acquiring property or funding a business; it is a structured pathway to building assets that can provide income, stability, and opportunity for decades. Backed by programs supported by the U.S. Small Business Administration, these loans allow disciplined borrowers to transition from earning income to owning assets, and from owning assets to creating a legacy.

Generational wealth begins with ownership. When you own commercial real estate, you control a tangible asset that has the potential to appreciate over time while generating consistent income. Unlike earned income, which is limited by time and effort, asset-based income can continue to grow independently. SBA loans make this transition accessible by reducing the capital required to acquire these assets, allowing more individuals to participate in ownership. The next layer of wealth creation is equity. Every payment made on an SBA loan reduces the principal balance, increasing your ownership stake in the property. At the same time, market appreciation can increase the value of the asset. This combination of principal reduction and appreciation creates a powerful compounding effect. Over time, equity becomes one of the most valuable components of your financial position, providing both security and opportunity.

Cash flow is the engine that sustains this system. A well-structured SBA deal generates income that exceeds its expenses, creating positive cash flow. This income can be used to support your lifestyle, reinvest in your business, or fund additional acquisitions. The goal is to build a portfolio where each asset contributes to overall income, creating a diversified and resilient financial structure.

Another key component of generational wealth is leverage. SBA loans allow you to control large assets with relatively small down payments, amplifying your ability to grow. While leverage must be used responsibly, it is one of the most effective tools for scaling your portfolio. By combining leverage with strong cash flow and disciplined management, you can accelerate your progress and achieve results that would be difficult to reach through savings alone.

Time is one of the most powerful factors in wealth creation. The longer you hold an asset, the more opportunity it has to appreciate and generate income. SBA loans, with their long-term structures, align well with this principle. By maintaining ownership over extended periods, you allow the compounding effects of equity and appreciation to work in your favor.

Diversification is another important element. Building wealth across multiple properties and income streams reduces risk and enhances stability. SBA financing allows you to acquire different types of assets, from owner-occupied properties to mixed-use buildings, creating a balanced portfolio that can withstand market fluctuations.

Another advanced concept is legacy planning. Generational wealth is not just about what you build—it is about how you transfer it. This involves structuring ownership in a way that allows assets to be passed on efficiently, minimizing taxes and ensuring continuity. This may include trusts, partnerships, or other legal structures designed to preserve wealth across generations.

Education is also a critical component of generational wealth. By sharing knowledge and involving family members in your business and investments, you create a foundation for continued success. Wealth is not just financial—it is also intellectual and strategic. Teaching the next generation how to manage and grow assets ensures that your efforts have a lasting impact.

Another key factor is reinvestment. Instead of consuming all of your income, successful borrowers reinvest a portion back into their portfolio. This creates a cycle of growth where each asset contributes to the acquisition of the next. Over time, this reinvestment strategy can significantly accelerate wealth accumulation.

Risk management remains essential, even at this advanced stage. Protecting your assets through insurance, maintaining reserves, and diversifying investments ensures that your wealth is preserved as well as grown. A strong risk management strategy provides stability and peace of mind.

Tax efficiency is another powerful tool. Commercial real estate offers several tax advantages, including depreciation and interest deductions, which can reduce taxable income and improve cash flow. Understanding and leveraging these benefits can significantly enhance overall returns.

As your portfolio grows, your focus shifts from individual deals to overall strategy. You begin to think in terms of systems, structures, and long-term outcomes. Each decision is evaluated based on how it contributes to your overall goals, creating a cohesive and intentional approach to wealth building. Ultimately, generational wealth is about creating freedom. It is about having the ability to make choices without financial constraints, to support your family, and to create opportunities for future generations. SBA commercial mortgage loans provide a pathway to achieve this by combining accessibility, structure, and scalability.

This chapter represents the culmination of everything you have learned. It is not just about understanding SBA financing—it is about using it to build a life of stability, opportunity, and impact. The strategies, tools, and principles are now in your hands.

The next step is to apply them.

Real-Life Math Example: Building Generational Wealth Step by Step

Let's walk through a comprehensive real-life scenario that demonstrates how SBA financing can be used to create generational wealth over time.

Imagine a borrower named Marcus who starts with a business generating $320,000 in annual net operating income. Marcus purchases his first property for $1,300,000 using an SBA loan with a 10% down payment of $130,000. The loan amount is $1,170,000 at 7% over 25 years, resulting in an annual debt service of approximately $99,600. Marcus leases out 30% of the property, generating $30,000 annually. This reduces his effective cost to $69,600. With a net income of $320,000, he has $250,400 remaining before taxes and reinvestment.

Over three years, Marcus grows his business, increasing net income to $420,000. The property appreciates to approximately $1,420,000. He refinances, accessing $180,000 in equity.

Marcus uses this $180,000 as a down payment on a second property valued at $1,900,000. The new loan has an annual debt service of $145,000, but the property generates $55,000 in rental income, reducing the effective cost.

Now Marcus owns two properties. His total income increases to $550,000, and his combined debt service remains manageable.

Over the next five years, both properties appreciate at 3% annually. The first property grows to approximately $1,650,000, and the second to approximately $2,200,000. Combined with principal reduction, Marcus builds over $900,000 in equity.

Marcus continues this process, acquiring a third and fourth property using the equity and cash flow generated from his existing portfolio. By year 12, he owns four properties with a combined value of over $7,000,000 and generates over $850,000 in annual net income. Let's break down the numbers further. Marcus's total annual debt service across all properties is approximately $420,000, while his income exceeds $850,000. This results in a DSCR of approximately 2.02, indicating a strong and sustainable financial position.

Additionally, his rental income exceeds $200,000 annually, providing diversification and stability.

As Marcus approaches retirement, his properties are largely paid down, and his cash flow increases significantly. He structures his assets in a way that allows them to be passed on to his children, creating a legacy that extends beyond his lifetime.

This example demonstrates how SBA financing can be used not just to build wealth, but to create a lasting impact. By starting with one property and applying a disciplined, strategic approach, Marcus is able to transform his financial future and provide opportunities for future generations.

The key takeaway is simple but powerful: ownership, consistency, and strategy create compounding results over time.

When combined with SBA commercial mortgage financing, these principles can turn ordinary opportunities into extraordinary outcomes.

Closing Thoughts

From Knowledge to Action — Your Path Forward

As you reach the end of *The SBA Commercial Mortgage Loan Mastery Series*, it is important to pause and reflect on the journey you have just completed. This series was not designed simply to provide information—it was designed to transform the way you think about financing, ownership, and wealth creation. You have moved from understanding basic loan concepts to mastering advanced strategies, from learning how to qualify for financing to structuring complex deals, and from analyzing individual transactions to building scalable systems. Now, everything comes down to one critical step: action.

The knowledge you have gained throughout this series gives you a significant advantage. You now understand how SBA commercial mortgage loans work, how they are structured, and how they can be used strategically to achieve your goals. You know how to evaluate opportunities, optimize cash flow, manage risk, and scale your portfolio. But knowledge without execution remains potential. The true value of this series lies in how you apply what you have learned.

One of the most important shifts you must make is moving from a mindset of consumption to a mindset of creation. Instead of constantly seeking more information, focus on implementing what you already know. The fundamentals you have learned are enough to get started. You do not need to wait for the perfect deal, the perfect timing, or the perfect conditions. Progress comes from taking consistent, calculated steps forward.

Your first deal is often the most challenging—not because it is the most complex, but because it requires you to step outside of your comfort zone. There will always be uncertainty, questions, and risks. However, the strategies outlined in this series are designed to minimize those risks and provide a clear framework for decision-making. Trust the process, rely on the principles you have learned, and take action with confidence.

As you begin, focus on building a strong foundation. This includes organizing your financials, strengthening your credit, and developing relationships with lenders and advisors. Preparation creates momentum. When you are ready, opportunities become easier to recognize and act upon. The more prepared you are, the more confident you will feel in your decisions.

Remember that success in SBA commercial mortgage financing is not about speed—it is about consistency. Each deal you complete builds your experience, strengthens your financial position, and expands your opportunities. Over time, these incremental gains compound into significant results. The goal is not to achieve everything at once, but to create a system that produces results repeatedly.

Another important principle is patience. Real estate and business ownership are long-term strategies. While there may be moments of rapid growth, the most significant gains often occur over time through appreciation, equity buildup, and reinvestment. By maintaining a long-term perspective, you can make decisions that prioritize sustainability and growth rather than short-term gains.

Challenges are inevitable, but they are also opportunities for growth. Every deal will present its own set of obstacles, whether related to financing, operations, or market conditions. The key is to approach these challenges with a problem-solving mindset. Each obstacle you overcome strengthens your skills and prepares you for more complex opportunities in the future.

Another critical factor is discipline. Financial success requires consistent decision-making aligned with your goals. This includes managing cash flow, maintaining reserves, and avoiding unnecessary risks. Discipline ensures that your growth is sustainable and that your portfolio remains resilient in changing conditions.

As your portfolio grows, your focus will naturally shift from individual transactions to overall strategy. You will begin to think in terms of systems, efficiency, and scalability. This is where the true power of SBA financing becomes evident. It allows you to build a structured approach to acquiring and managing assets, creating a foundation for long-term success.

Relationships will play an increasingly important role in your journey. Building strong connections with lenders, brokers, contractors, and advisors can open doors to new opportunities and provide valuable insights. These relationships are not just transactional—they are partnerships that support your growth and success.

Education is an ongoing process. While this series provides a comprehensive foundation, the market continues to evolve, and new opportunities will emerge. Staying informed and adaptable ensures that you remain competitive and capable of navigating changes. However, always remember that action is the priority. Learning should support execution, not replace it.

One of the most rewarding aspects of this journey is the ability to create impact beyond yourself. As you build wealth and stability, you gain the capacity to support your family, contribute to your community, and create opportunities for others. This is the true essence of generational wealth—not just financial success, but the ability to make a lasting difference. It is also important to recognize that your journey will be unique. While the principles in this series provide a framework, your path will be shaped by your goals, your experiences, and your decisions. Embrace this individuality and use it to create a strategy that aligns with your vision.

As you move forward, keep your focus on progress. Every step you take, no matter how small, brings you closer to your goals. Celebrate your successes, learn from your challenges, and continue refining your approach. Growth is a continuous process, and each experience contributes to your development.

The most important takeaway from this series is that you are in control of your financial future. SBA commercial mortgage financing provides the tools, but it is your decisions and actions that determine the outcome. By applying the strategies you have learned, you can create opportunities, build assets, and achieve a level of financial independence that many believe is out of reach.

This is not the end of your journey—it is the beginning. You now have the knowledge, the strategies, and the framework needed to move forward with confidence. The next step is yours to take.

Take action. Stay consistent. Think long-term.

And most importantly, build something that lasts.

How to Get a Personalized SBA Commercial Mortgage Review

If you found this book helpful, you may want to see how these strategies apply to your specific financial situation.

SBA commercial mortgage financing is highly customized—your business income, financial statements, credit profile, property type, industry, and long-term goals all play a role in determining what you qualify for and how your loan should be structured.

Every borrower's situation is different. Your revenue trends, business model, tax returns, debt obligations, ownership structure, and the type of commercial property you are purchasing, refinancing, or building all impact your options. The strategies and examples in this book are designed to teach you how SBA commercial mortgage loans work—but your actual loan approval, terms, and structure can only be determined by analyzing your real financial profile.

If you would like a no-obligation SBA Commercial Mortgage review, you can request one here:

Email: info@FinibiMortgage.com

A licensed mortgage broker will review your business financials, income structure, credit profile, and goals, and explain what SBA financing options may be available to you—including:

• SBA 7(a) commercial mortgage loans• SBA 504 fixed-rate commercial real estate financing• Owner-occupied property qualification strategies• Business acquisition with real estate financing• Commercial refinance and cash-out strategies• Construction and expansion loan structuring• Advanced SBA deal structuring to maximize approval

No cost. No pressure. No obligation.

Sincerely,

Joseph G. Correa

Finibi Mortgage Inc.

Licensed Mortgage Broker

About the Author

Joseph G. Correa is a licensed mortgage broker and the founder of Finibi Mortgage, a Florida-based brokerage specializing in SBA commercial mortgage loans, non-QM lending, and strategic real estate financing solutions for business owners, entrepreneurs, and investors.

With more than two decades of experience in mortgage lending, underwriting, and deal structuring, Joseph has helped thousands of clients secure financing for commercial real estate, business acquisitions, and complex transactions using both traditional and alternative lending strategies.

Unlike traditional loan officers who focus only on basic qualification, Joseph's approach emphasizes **cash flow analysis, deal structuring, and strategic financing**. He believes that business owners should not be limited by rigid lending formulas, but instead empowered by understanding how to structure deals that align with lender guidelines and maximize approval potential.

Joseph is widely recognized for his expertise in:

• SBA 7(a) and SBA 504 commercial mortgage loans• Owner-occupied commercial real estate financing• Business acquisition with real estate structuring• Commercial refinance and cash flow optimization• Construction and expansion financing• Advanced loan structuring and approval strategy

Through his education platform, Finibi Academy, Joseph has trained tens of thousands of students worldwide in mortgage strategy, real estate investing, credit optimization, and financial independence.

He created the *SBA Commercial Mortgage Loan Mastery Series* to provide a clear, step-by-step roadmap for borrowers and professionals who want to understand, qualify for, and scale commercial real estate using SBA financing.

His mission is simple:

To help business owners use strategic financing to acquire assets, build cash flow, and create long-term wealth.

When he is not structuring loans or writing, Joseph works with clients across the United States to design customized SBA financing strategies aligned with their business goals and growth plans.

The SBA Commercial Mortgage Loan Mastery Series Roadmap

The Complete Guide to Using SBA Financing to Build Commercial Real Estate and Business Wealth

The purpose of *The SBA Commercial Mortgage Loan Mastery Series* is to give business owners, investors, and mortgage professionals the exact strategies used by lenders and underwriters—translated into simple, practical steps you can apply in real life.

This series takes you from beginner to advanced mastery of how to qualify, structure, and scale commercial real estate and business financing using SBA mortgage loans.

Each book builds on the last. You are not just learning how to get approved—you are learning how to control your approvals and scale your opportunities.

Book 1 — SBA Commercial Mortgage Loan Fundamentals Understand how SBA mortgage programs work, including 7(a) and 504 loans, and how to qualify.

Book 2 — Getting Approved for an SBA Commercial Mortgage Loan Learn step-by-step strategies to meet lender requirements and secure funding.

Book 3 — Owner-Occupied Property Financing with SBA Loans Learn how to buy or refinance your business property using SBA financing.

Book 4 — Buying a Business and Real Estate with SBA Financing Acquire a business and its property in one structured transaction.

Book 5 — SBA 7(a) Mortgage Loan Strategies Master flexible loan structures for business and real estate funding.

Book 6 — SBA 504 Mortgage Loans for Commercial Real Estate Use long-term fixed-rate financing for large property acquisitions.

Book 7 — Refinancing Commercial Debt with SBA Loans Lower payments, improve cash flow, and restructure existing debt.

Book 8 — SBA Loans for Construction and Expansion Build, renovate, and scale commercial properties with structured financing.

Book 9 — SBA Loan Requirements, Rates, and Structures Understand how to compare options and choose the best loan.

Book 10 — Advanced SBA Commercial Mortgage Structuring Engineer approvals and maximize leverage using expert strategies.

This series is designed to move you from:

Understanding → Execution → Scaling → Mastery

By the end, you will not just know how to qualify—you will know how to structure, analyze, and scale deals like a professional.

Educational & Financial Disclaimer

The *SBA Commercial Mortgage Loan Mastery Series* is intended for educational and informational purposes only.

This content is designed to help readers understand SBA commercial mortgage lending, real estate financing strategies, and business acquisition concepts. It is not financial, legal, tax, or investment advice.

Joseph G. Correa and Live Stronger Faster are not acting as your personal financial advisor, attorney, accountant, or mortgage professional through this publication.

SBA loan programs, underwriting guidelines, interest rates, and lender requirements may change at any time and vary by lender.

All examples in this series are for illustration purposes only and do not guarantee approval or results.

Always consult with licensed professionals before making financial decisions.

Risk Disclosure

SBA commercial mortgage lending and real estate investing involve risk.

Business performance, income stability, interest rate changes, market conditions, and lender guidelines can all impact loan approval and financial outcomes.

Borrowing against real estate or using leverage increases both potential returns and risk.

Failure to repay a loan may result in foreclosure and loss of property.

Cash flow, rental income, appreciation, and business performance are not guaranteed.

All strategies presented in this series are educational and must be evaluated based on your individual financial situation.

You are solely responsible for your financial decisions.

www.ingramcontent.com/pod-product-compliance
Lightning Source LLC
LaVergne TN
LVHW022223200926
848481LV00006B/2092
* 9 7 9 8 2 9 5 8 1 7 2 8 1 *